You Think You Are Doing Well?

Become a Winner with Customer-centric Process Leadership

JANNE OHTONEN

COMPANIES, ORGANIZATIONS, INSTITUTIONS, AND INDUSTRY PUBLICATIONS: Quantity discounts are available on bulk purchases of this book for reselling, educational purposes, subscription incentives, gifts, sponsorship, or fundraising. Special books or book excerpts can also be created to fit specific needs such as private labeling with your logo on the cover and a message from a VIP printed inside. For more information please contact us through http://bit.ly/52weeksbook or 52weeks@ohtonen.fi

This book is sold with the understanding that neither the author nor the publisher is engaged in rendering legal, accounting, or financial services. The author and publisher specifically disclaim any liability, loss, or risk, personal or otherwise, which is incurred as a consequence, directly or indirectly, of the use and application of any of the strategies in this book.

First published in Helsinki, Finland in MMXIII by Glamonor LP.
2nd edition published MMXIV.

Visit http://bit.ly/52weeksbook for FREE infographics and videos!

ISBN: 978-952-68055-0-4 (paperback)
ISBN: 978-952-68055-1-1 (PDF)
ISBN: 978-952-68055-2-8 (EPUB)

DEDICATION

To all those people who serve others.

PROCEEDS OF THIS BOOK
ARE GIVEN TO CHARITY

With a small donation and big faith, John Kirkby started Christians Against Poverty (CAP) in 1996. He believed God was calling him to sacrifice his career in finance and use his knowledge of the industry to help the poor.

Since then, CAP has rapidly grown its centre network and provides the best debt help service to those with the very least. CAP started running Money Courses in partnership with local churches to help people budget, save and prevent debt. Our vision is to help answer the national problem of debt by opening a CAP Debt Centre and running a CAP Money Course in every town and city in the UK so anyone can receive CAP's life changing help.

Proceeds from this book are donated to CAP charity.

CONTENTS

ACKNOWLEDGMENTS

Made it all possible

Jesus: Our Saviour and Lord.

Supported me on the way

Hanna Norvanto-Ohtonen, Daniel Ohtonen, Arja Ohtonen, Jarmo Ohtonen, Miika J. Norvanto, Jukka Norvanto, Liisa Norvanto, Elisa Norvanto, Pirita Norvanto, Mira Ohtonen, Mikael Jaakkola, Minna Karjalainen, Mikko Karjalainen, Toni Karjalainen, Nea Karjalainen, Miral Ismail, Tommi Hännikkälä, Liisa Määttä, Petri Määttä, Harri Kulmala, Tuukka Heinonen, John C. Maxwell, Life Church Cuffley, Robin Sharma, Reint Jan Holterman, Gerry Robert, Paul Martinelli, Kevin Clark, Philip Coffin, Laura Doyle, Lizzie Johns, Kristina Priecelova and the rest of my family, friends and colleagues.

Thank you for these websites for sharing the words

http://www.linkedin.com/in/janneohtonen
http://www.facebook.com/successconsultant
http://twitter.com/Ohtonen
http://www.bpmleader.com/author/johtonen
http://www.processexcellencenetwork.com/contributors/3969-janne-ohtonen/
http://live.icmgworld.com/index.php/askthearchitects/317-janne-ohtonen/profile.html
http://customerthink.com/author/janneohtonen/
http://bit.ly/52weeksbook

"WHEN ONE HAS FINISHED BUILDING ONE'S HOUSE, ONE SUDDENLY REALISES THAT IN THE PROCESS ONE HAS LEARNED SOMETHING THAT ONE REALLY NEEDED TO KNOW IN THE WORST WAY—BEFORE ONE BEGAN."

– Friedrich Nietzsche

INTRODUCTION

This book has been written to help you to develop both your personal leadership and your business skills with each passing week. Even though this book may initially seem like a random collection of wisdom, it is based on the experience I have accumulated over 10 years of working as a professional business coach. The world has become a complex place and many kinds of demands are placed on the people who work in decision-making positions. This book seeks to help you to move forward on your path of personal growth towards better leadership and business improvement skills. What you can expect from this book is a compilation of thought-provoking ideas and reflective questions that will hopefully trigger your mind to generate insight that adds value to your life. In this second edition I have made improvements based on the feedback I have received since the publishing of the first edition. Please, keep on sending your feedback to revise the future editions.

I have included a suggested list of additional reading that will provide you with more detailed information about various topics discussed in this book. Reading around different topics will give you ideas that you might not get from traditional sources. And for that reason I recommend you read one chapter every week and concentrate on the thoughts it provokes in you so that you can use the results to improve something in your personal or work life. Write your thoughts down to empty space reserved at the end of each week.

Over a decade ago, I began a career as a software programmer, but came to the conclusion over the years that plain technology is boring, because it will not help people unless people have some need they can fulfil with the technology. I decided to make a change and I became an enterprise architect. I started designing new more efficient ways of doing business and optimise processes. It was useful since it enabled me to align technology with the work people do. But still it felt like something was missing. That is why I educated myself to become a business coach. Like John C. Maxwell says, "All rise and fall with leadership", top management support to improve business performance is key for companies to succeed in a long run. All of these topics that I have described within this book, one for each week, have been used to improve myself or the business that I work for. So in that sense this thought leadership has been tried with real-life cases. I hope that this book will give you several useful insights over the next 52 weeks also.

You can read this book in several ways. It has been designed so that there is one theme for each week of the year and you can start reading it from the current week number or you can read it in sequence, by using this current week as week number one. Either way, over the next 52 weeks you will have touched upon some of the important topics in the field of Leadership and customer-centric Business Process Management (BPM). I have written these themes to be short and to the point, so that you will use less time reading and more time thinking. It is not so important what exactly I have written here, but what ideas you produce each week during and after reading these texts. So, be sensitive to yourself and listen to your intuition. Try to find what you could do better this week and work concisely towards those goals.

If you want to make your own notes about any of the topics, at the end of each topic there is space for this under the text "Write down your own thoughts here". Do not worry about marking this book as those thoughts will be the most valuable outcome you can get by following this book. You can download more resources from http://bit.ly/52weeksbook.

If you have any questions or you would like to discuss with me regarding any topic, I would love to connect with you at LinkedIn and continue our discussion there. Please connect with me for further discussion here http://linkedin.com/in/janneohtonen

FOREWORD BY REINT JAN HOLTERMAN

Panta rhei, or "everything flows". These words have been assigned to the Greek philosopher Heraclitus, indicating that everything is susceptible to change. This still holds true, 2500 years after these words were first spoken.

Organisations are constantly changing, under pressures of market demands, competitive forces, technological inventions, and new legislation. In response to these external impacts on their business and value proposition, organisations adapt their way of working—i.e. they adapt their business processes. What is most fascinating (at least to me personally) is the explanations as to why some organisations are doing so much better in changing their processes than others. Why do well-performing organisations—profit as much as non-profit—know how to adapt their processes swiftly and adequately, in comparison to their weaker performing counterparts that lag behind or disappear completely after a while?

Answering this question was, for me, the main reason to start an on-line community for Business Process Management (BPM) professionals in 2011. Experts from all around the world contribute their views and opinions about BPM, process workflow automation, process improvement, change management, case management, process analytics, and related topics. This community entitled *BPM Leader* operates as a strictly non-commercial knowledge-sharing platform. Thought leaders freely express ideas that eventually all connect to the starting premise: why are some organisations doing better than others in relation to the adaptation to the ever-changing world?

One of these thought leaders that became actively involved in the BPM Leader community as author and visionary was Janne Ohtonen. With over 35 contributions, he quickly became the best-read blogger in our community. Sometimes thought-provoking, sometimes eye-opening, his contributions were always well written as well as thoroughly researched and supported by his scientific research and Ph.D. work in the field of BPM. So it was no surprise for me to hear he has also been working on a book to further elaborate on these topics and to explore the relationship between process management, leadership and customer centricity. It is an honour that Janne asked me to write this foreword to his book.

This book consists of 52 articles, one for each week throughout the year. It articulates, in a very concise and clear fashion, a number of best practices for business leaders to adapt their organisations in response to the new behaviours of customers. Today's customers expect to be treated personally, instantly, and through their own preferred channel—be it on-line or off-line. They now have the means to impose this on organisations, being members of a socially hyper-connected world and with all information right at their fingertips. Organisations simply need to modify their practices to this new type of customer, not (only) by opening an on-line store or a Twitter account, but by changing their mind-sets, behaviours and leadership styles to become truly customer-centric. They need to implement customer-centric process leadership. How? Just read on, as that is what this book is all about!

So even if you think you are doing well already, are you a winner in your own markets? If you are, it will be interesting to reflect upon the thoughts presented in this book, and read about what you can do to *stay* a winner too. For all others who are not (yet) the winner in their market: you will discover new approaches to help you to gradually become one in this must-read book!

Amersfoort (Netherlands), 5 November 2013

Reint Jan Holterman

Founder & Publisher, BPM Leader

(For more information on BPM Leader, please visit www.bpmleader.com)

WEEK 1: ARE YOU STILL WORKING WITH OUTDATED BUSINESS METHODS?

Many of the world's leading companies have come to realise that only when their customers are successful, will they also be successful (for example, Google, Apple, Microsoft, IBM and, in particular, Zappos). In pursuit of their market leadership, they not only need to spend time looking into their businesses to know how things are getting done (BPM, Lean, Six Sigma, etc.), but also looking outward to get a deep understanding of their customers (Voice of Customer) and what they really need (Outside-In Customer centricity).

Business processes have indeed come a long way from their humble beginnings of the early Industrial Revolution and Adam Smith's '*Wealth of Nations*'. He was one of the first people to describe business process in 1776 as a new way for doing work in a Scottish pin factory. He outlined the production methods and created one of the first objective and measureable enterprise process designs. The consequence of '*labour division*' in Smith's example resulted in the same number of workers making over 200 times as many pins as they had prior to the introduction of Smith's way of working.

Adam Smith participated in a labour revolution that transformed the business world. He lived in a time of political change, founding Americas' industrialisation, and a new optimism that rose from the restraints of the past. During this time, the foundation was laid that established a way of working that has survived and thrived until the present day.

And yet now, more than ever, is a time to take a careful look at the past to guide the way for not only surviving the current economic turmoil, but also to prepare us to thrive in the twenty-first century business world order, where the customer has become central to everything we do.

Leading global corporations (for example, Amazon, BMW and Zara) are now evolving their tried and tested approaches into methods suited to the changed challenges of customer disloyalty, globalisation, IT innovation and the educated customer. That is the essence of what we experts call Outside-In or Customer centricity. It is time to change Adam Smith's views and update the business methods for this century.

Outside-In thinking can be summarised by the statement: "*the customer experience is the process you should be managing*". We can no longer work out of organisation-centric approaches (called Inside-Out) to create a sustainable competitive advantage. We have to extend our scope and embrace a broader view of optimising processes by understanding, managing and developing customer expectations and the associated experience. We need to articulate Successful Customer Outcomes (SCOs) and let those guide our product and service development as we move beyond the limiting scope of factory-minded hierarchical thinking. Is your organisation using organisation-centric methods to manage customer expectations? If the answer is yes, then how well has it worked for you? My guess is that there is still a lot to do to change your business into one which is truly customer-centric, i.e. Outside-In. Customers change all the time, and so should your business.

Foregoers of customer centricity estimate that most organisations could reduce their cost base by a further 20–40% without any reduction in revenue or service level and this estimate also applies to companies who have already optimised multiple times already. The impact of such change will of course significantly affect profitability. The reduction in costs (without impacting on revenue or competitive position) will create only short-term gains (by short-term I mean two or three years). Companies espousing Lean and Six Sigma, such as Motorola and GE, who focus on cost cutting without revenue improvement ultimately fall into business decline.

Some see Outside-In as the end for other approaches such as Business Process Management, Business Process Reengineering, Total Quality Management and Lean Six Sigma. This narrow and simplistic view does not acknowledge the stepping stones available to embrace the new customer-centric order. In fact, the foundation of our future is always laid on the lessons of the past with the innovators who recognise the need to evolve leading that charge. Lean and Six Sigma still have their place in optimising manufacturing processes. Nonetheless, for service and support processes, Outside-In approaches will bring more significant results.

This year, those who seize the moment and push forward their approaches into the new business world ruled by customer centricity will reap the benefits. The process of aligning every aspect of the organisation's operations to the achievement of the SCOs drives out non-contributory work and optimises the cost base. It is precisely the achievement of these fundamentals that delivers the sort of turnaround figures stated earlier.

There are a number of Outside-In change methods emerging, but most are still in their infancy. One of the most advanced at the moment is a method called CEI (Customer Experience Innovation). In its basic form, the Customer Experience Innovation Method assesses and aligns the business using the following approach:

- Create process activity map: identify each step and activity in the chosen process.
- Evaluate current process diagnostics and identify:
  o customer interactions/touchpoints to the process;
  o internal handovers;
  o business rules and decision-making points.
- Develop SCOs, which answer the question: why does this process deserve to exist?

- Perform Risk Assessment both from the organisation's and the customer's perspective to prioritise the change efforts.
- Develop an action and change project plan.
- Lead the change programme and see the results for yourself.

The SCO (Successful Customer Outcome) understanding and development process can also be used as a strategy or innovation tool and will uncover business opportunities that neither company nor customer had ever considered previously.

The evaluation of process diagnostics is the first step of process alignment. Process views are different from those used in previous generation methodologies, in that they look at a process starting with customer interaction points. The process of understanding and delivering to the SCO framework, underpinned by an alignment of everything the company does to its customer achievement, defines a future state that the organisation can move to in less than a year.

Summary

We are still working with methods that are hundreds of years old even though the world around us has changed significantly. The industrial ways (founded by Adam Smith) to optimise business do not work for service businesses in the same way as it does for manufacturing, but still many companies are using those methods and struggling. Using more customer-centric approaches, such as Outside-In, will bring significant benefits to cost reduction, revenue and customer service. There are practical ways to harness this power, such as the Customer Experience Innovation Method.

Here are some reflective questions you can ask yourself to promote your thinking:
- How could you optimise business processes in your organisation?
- How could you get the most effective methods to develop your business?
- How could you benefit from a standardised way to develop your business?
- How could using the Customer Experience Innovation Method benefit your organisation?
- How could your organisation benefit from using organisation-centric methods to manage customer expectations?

Write down your own thoughts here:

WEEK 2: WHAT IS BUSINESS PROCESS MANAGEMENT?

As a concept, process management is almost one hundred years old. It has been seen as a real challenger for product control concepts. The basic idea of business processes and their management has been to create value for the customer through activities in an organisation and to fulfil other strategies such as producing returns to stakeholders. Development of process methodologies started in the 1970s and Business Process Reengineering (BPR) and other methods were introduced in the 1990s onwards. Dr. Palmberg has done research on the history and development of Business Process Management (BPM). She came to a conclusion based on an extensive literature review, that there is no one clear definition for the term '*Business Process Management*'. She states that it is to be seen more as a collection of certain matters rather than as one clear term. Still, process management has stayed on the surface of business management concepts throughout the years. The basic definition of processes can be depicted in the following figure.

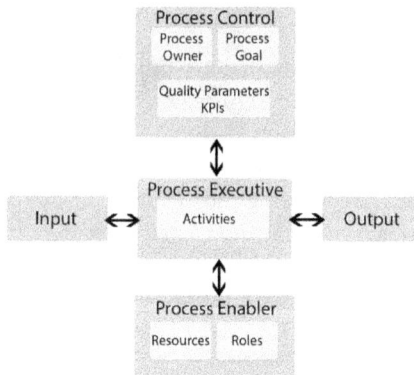

BPM is about managing those processes with a wider perspective, defined by the strategy and mission of the organisation. BPM should be planned after considering all aspects of the particular business so that it will be the appropriate up-to-date system. Regular inspection and evaluation at different levels of process management is needed to improve the workflow and also to enhance the work output of a business. If proper BPM is not carried out, then those companies will not be able to attain their potential output. In such companies, the risk management will be poor, and they will be more prone to pitfalls and future losses. This can even lead the business into a state of collapse.

Nowadays, software tools are commonly used to aid BPM activities. These tools are known as BPM systems. These software tools carry out suitable process analysis so that negative consequences are nullified. BPM systems make the designing and implementation of all business management processes cheap, easy and efficient. The purpose of BPM is to:

- Align the process to strategic objectives of an organisation.
- Control and improve processes.
- Remove barriers between organisational silos, also known as business units, departments, teams, etc.
- Identify opportunities to use technology.
- Improve organisational effectiveness.
- Improve business performance.

This is one view on BPM, but there are many others also. However, BPM is just not enough today, because it still has that burden of Adam Smith's industrial way of thinking, which does not respond to the desires of the modern day customers. Business processes exist to provide added value to customers; the only way to do that is to know what customers really need from your business and then you can use BPM to optimise your processes to deliver what is required. If you do not have that profound reason for an organisation to exist guiding your BPM projects, they will be useless because there is no point in optimising something that is not needed.

Summary

Business Process Management (BPM) is not a well understood term. Sometimes it is an excuse to downsize a company or to hide technology projects. BPM is about managing all the business processes of an organisation in a meaningful way to deliver successful customer outcomes. Sometimes this may mean downsizing or having new IT systems, but that should never be the goal. The overall purpose of BPM is to improve organisational effectiveness and business performance.

Here are some reflective questions you can ask yourself to promote your thinking:

- Do you have BPM in your organisation?
  - o If you have, is it aligned to optimise processes that are really needed to provide added value to your customers?
  - o If you do not have BPM in place, what benefits could you get from optimising your processes actively?
- What does BPM mean to you?
- How can you get the benefits BPM has to offer into your organisation?

Write down your own thoughts here:

WEEK 3: WASTE FROM A CUSTOMER'S PERSPECTIVE

In today's marketplace, every organisation must become more efficient or the business is going to be outperformed by the competition. When it comes to business processes, eliminating waste is very important. That waste, also known as unnecessary work, may assume one of the following forms.

Overproduction and Inventory

Both old and new organisations easily fall into the trap of overproduction, with some producing goods before there are buyers and others producing more goods than there is demand for. Both situations are bad for the organisation, especially from an internal perspective. From a customer's perspective, overproduction might lead to shorter delivery times and lower market prices. A customer-oriented perspective might indicate that customers get the products in the timescale in which they need them and the price is balanced with the value it yields to the customers. Overproduction is something to be avoided, but at the same we need to make sure that we have the right amount of goods in inventory to be delivered within the timeframe that customers expect to receive them. Are you measuring the expected and realised delivery times to your customers and the deviation between the two?

Waiting

As we all know, waiting for something or someone in a process is costly. While waiting, some people might not have anything to do and partly manufactured parts need to be stored somewhere. Also switching from one process or activity to another wastes employees time (due to reorientation to the new activity). From a customer's perspective, it undervalues customers' time, since the organisation is not able to design their processes and inventories so that there are no ineffectual waiting times that delay the process. In some cases, business rules can cause situations where there are unnecessary waiting times. Have you evaluated all your business rules to ensure that are they still valid?

Processing

This is one of the most customer-facing phases in manufacturing, even though many organisations do not seem to think so. This is where time is taken, quality is put into products, value is created for the customer and pretty much all the work within an organisation is undertaken. It is not enough to measure all the nuts and bolts of the process from an internal perspective, but we need to also evaluate the processes from a customer-oriented perspective. That means seeking the answers to questions such as: "Is this something customers really need?" or "Does this process contribute to successful customer outcomes?". With a customer-oriented perspective it is possible to extend traditional Lean and Six Sigma thinking to question the overall reasons for certain processes to exist in an organisation. That will lead to increased revenue, reduced costs and improved customer service simultaneously. From a merely internal perspective, that is hard to come by.

Correction

When everything goes smoothly everyone is happy, but those are not the times when an organisation is really evaluated. The true measure is in those moments when something fails. And as we know, corrections cost a lot. Thus, an organisation should strive to make as few mistakes as possible. However, since perfection is hard to achieve, an organisation should have proper corrective methods in place. From a customer-oriented perspective, an organisation should always seek the cause of an error rather than the effect. Furthermore, endeavour to make sure that you as an organisation are the one that notices the error rather than the customer. It sounds very obvious, but do you have clear measures and plans for reacting to reclamations and other customer feedback? Are you measuring those with the same enthusiasm as any manufacturing mistakes detected internally? And foremost, have you linked that information together?

Reducing waste in your processes

If you have inefficiency in your processes, you might be making more products than you need, having people waiting for turns in the process or you are not fixing mistakes efficiently. In many cases, you may be doing all the aforementioned things right, but you are missing the customer perspective from your process optimisation efforts, and that will prevent you from creating even better business. Here are some ideas for reducing waste in your processes:

- *Sifting.* Internal (Six Sigma/Lean) perspective recommends removing things from the work area that are not required in order to do the job. The customer-oriented perspective suggests that getting rid of all the work that does not directly contribute to producing successful customer outcomes.
- *Sorting.* Organise tools and materials. Also evaluate how those that remain contribute to creating value for customers.
- *Standardising.* Eliminate random elements that slow production, while at the same time creating an environment that enables people to present their ideas on improving the processes. Standardise your processes for manufacturing successful customer outcomes (products

are just a medium for that). And while doing this, keep in mind where the process starts and ends for your customers, not just for your organisation.

- *Self-discipline.* Insist upon consistent performance. Make the customer everyone's business across your organisation.

Summary

First, it is essential to evaluate what your customer really needs from your organisation, and then plan improvements to the process, before applying the changes. Check to see if it worked with both internal and customer-oriented measures. Then, based on the results, act to improve the process further. It is important not to do this all from an internal perspective only; have the best experts evaluate what you do: the customers.

Here are some reflective questions to ask yourself to promote your thinking:

- Is your production (of goods or services) balanced both from internal and customer perspectives?
- Have you evaluated how much time your customers waste waiting for you? How can you change that?
- Have you evaluated how much time you waste waiting on customers? How can you change that?
- Have you evaluated how everything you do contributes to successful customer outcomes?
- Are you reducing waste in your processes from internal or customer perspectives? How has it worked out for you?
- Have you evaluated and documented who your customers are; why are they your customers and what needs do they have?

Write down your own thoughts here:

WEEK 4: OUTSIDE-IN PERSPECTIVE ON LEAN ORGANISATIONAL CULTURE

Lean organisational culture helps manufacturing organisations to stay on track with Lean methodology in the long run. The Lean culture is critical for sustainability and to change it, you have to change your management system. If you stop following through with Lean practices because things seem stable and under control, it is certain that you will soon face unstable and out-of-control processes. Lean management culture is crucial to the success of Lean production, because it both sustains and extends the gains from establishing Lean procedures.

Outside-In (customer-centric) perspective expands the traditional way of perceiving Lean, which is extremely internally focused on an organisation's activities. Outside means looking at the organisation with customers' eyes. Thus, Outside-In refers to improving an organisation's internal functions with a customer-oriented perspective. Let's discuss how Lean organisational culture, i.e. the Lean management system, can be extended with Outside-In perspective. I will explain the idea of Outside-In Lean in more detail later in this book, but in essence it is about expanding the traditional Lean culture with customer orientation.

To achieve the maximum effect for organisational improvement, implement your Lean management system extended with Outside-In perspective as early in your Lean conversion process as possible. Use the techniques related to Outside-In to maximise the value your processes produce to customers and then Lean techniques to optimise those processes from an internal perspective.

The basic outline for creating a Lean culture or management system is quite simple. However, keep in mind that even simple systems require close attention and maintenance to run smoothly. You should build your Lean culture on the following essential elements: make the customer everyone's business, standardise work for managers, have daily accountability, and require discipline.

Make the customer everyone's business

The customer is the very reason for an organisation to exist. There is no need for Lean process management without customers, because without them there would not be any processes to manage. Therefore, make the customer everyone's business, because if their wage is paid by the customer, they should think about how what they do contributes to the successful customer outcomes that the organisation should be producing. Getting rid of useless processes is more effective than tweaking them.

Standardise work for managers

People are not machines, so it is impossible to standardise everything. Managers and especially leaders should have a high awareness of what is going on around them. However, it is possible to standardise some aspects of managers' work to make sure that everyone delivers within the same levels. Standardised work (for example, task lists) presents a clearly stated recipe for management, making it easier to evaluate managers' effectiveness. Those standards should not be solely built on internal tasks; it should also include the evaluation of processes from an Outside-In perspective.

Require discipline

When thinking about your Lean management system, consider a motorcycle metaphor. Standardised work is its 'engine' and your daily accountability process represents its 'gas throttle and steering rod'. Discipline is the 'fuel' that keeps the motorcycle running and your customer is the 'driver'. Having all the elements of your Lean management system in place is not enough, because each has to be observed individually for the system as a whole to work.

Summary

For the Outside-In Lean methodology to thrive in your organisation, it must permeate your culture and earn top management's support in the same way as any process improvement endeavour. Since both Outside-In and Lean are specific ways of thinking, helping others to adopt these mindsets is a big part of ensuring success. Transforming your organisation requires considerable effort. There is wide variation between the traditional and new ways, so a conversion requires you to re-educate everyone in the organisation, beginning with yourself. As an Outside-In Lean advocate, you are asking people to adopt habits and practices that are the exact opposite of what they are accustomed to doing.

Here are some reflective questions you can ask yourself to promote your thinking:
- Have you become sloppy in following practice since things have been going well?
- How is the customer included in your process management initiatives?
- Is the customer everyone's business in your organisation? If the answer is no, should they be?
- Are your leaders sensitive to each current situation?

Write down your own thoughts here:

WEEK 5: DMAIC FROM THE CUSTOMER'S VIEWPOINT

The goal of Six Sigma is to achieve consistent, reliable, repeatable performance in areas that affect effectiveness and efficiency. Effectiveness measures how the customers' needs or wants are met and efficiency measures the cost of meeting the customers' needs or wants. Let's go through DMAIC (Define, Measure, Analyse, Implement, Control) from a customer's viewpoint.

Six Sigma has five steps, summed up by the acronym DMAIC. Titles are the traditional way of thinking in Six Sigma and the explanation below is in regard to the customer perspective.

1) Define the company's processes and customer needs

Processes are the ways that companies take inputs, add value and deliver outputs. Every business organisation is all about their customers, every governmental office is all about serving citizens and every not-for-profit organisation is all about serving people related to their mission. Thus, we can say that the customer experience is the process for every organisation in one way or another. For the customer, process inputs are their true needs, added value is the way that those needs are taken care of, and delivered outputs are customers with fulfilled needs. It is not about what customers want, it is about what they need. And for customers, processes are the ways that organisations take care of their needs.

2) Measure process effectiveness (meeting the customer's needs and wants) and efficiency (the cost of meeting the customer's needs or wants)

How do you feel when you are sent a customer satisfaction questionnaire with 50 questions? Or you are asked to answer a questionnaire that doesn't really ask anything you would like to answer? Well, your customers will feel the same way as you do in that situation. Customers actually want the measurement of process effectiveness to be as invisible as possible to them, but at the same time, as efficient as possible. You shouldn't ask the customers how long they waited in a queue, because from their viewpoint you should know that. You should also know how long they are willing to wait in a queue. If you want to conduct a feedback questionnaire, it should ask only: will you use/buy our services/products again? Would you recommend our services/products to your friends/family? And then as appropriate, a "why not" question if the respondent says no. You should figure out the rest without continuously bothering the customers.

3) Analyse the data in an attempt to identify the causes of variation in the process

From an organisation's internal perspective, it is important to analyse the variation in processes. From a customer's viewpoint, they are actually the first ones noticing the variation, long before your measurement systems, because they will suffer from the effects. The more you can prevent variation, the better. But it is not only about measuring and analysing; it is more about reacting to that variance. Organisations need to deal with the effects and remove the cause. When things go wrong, your customers will expect you to do something about it. And the world's best organisations are working on that proactively; they will know and deal with the problem in real time for customers. For example, when thinking about IT systems, your customer should not be the first one noticing that your servers are down and they cannot access the system.

4) Improve the process by doing things differently

By differently, customers mean fulfilling their needs better. Statistical analysis of the processes is not enough to tell you how to improve processes from a customer experience perspective, especially if you have not measured the right things from the beginning. Try to find the optimum number of customer interactions and that will lead to increased revenue, reduced costs and improved customer service simultaneously.

5) Use control measures to make sure the improvements stay in force

Control the customer experience at all times. You have to make the customer everyone's business in your organisation, from top to bottom (in a hierarchical world) or from customer to outcome (in a process world).

Summary

As this week's chapter has shown, it is possible to visit process development methods from a customer perspective. That will significantly change how we use those methods to improve our organisation. Having a customer-centric perspective on Six Sigma's DMAIC is beneficial to the organisation, because it will shift the focus from internal activities to external outcomes, which will enable you to identify new revenue sources, decrease costs and improve customer service simultaneously.

Here are some reflective questions you can ask yourself to promote your thinking:
- Is your organisation thinking about the customer in every step of Six Sigma DMAIC?

- Do you evaluate every process's right to exist before optimising it?
- Do you measure the right things that provide successful customer outcomes?
- Do you control your processes based on the right measurements?

Write down your own thoughts here:

WEEK 6: WHAT KINDS OF SNAKES LIVE IN PROCESS PARADISE?

It would be nice if it were possible to have process improvement initiatives without any problems. However, that is not the world we live in. Process paradise can run into numerous problems. Watch out for these potential snakes hissing in your process garden.

"Step on the snake's tail and it will bite you."

The customers are the most important stakeholders of any organisation, because they pay for the organisation to exist. Do not step on the tail of that snake or it will bite you and release its venom. Process improvement should be used to provide better customer experiences.

"The culture of snakes."

Many people do not like change, but the culture of change is very important for process improvement. All the employees of your organisation must be convinced that they are in the change business. People who believe that process improvement is not their job create problems. It is impossible to retain old habits of working when the world around the organisation changes all the time due to globalisation, the Internet, technological advances, and so on.

"You cannot use a submarine to kill a snake."

Watch out for a mismatch between new methods or tools and the work. Remember to apply proper project management techniques to direct your Six Sigma initiative's scope, standards, schedule and levels of risk. Start with the end in mind.

"Focusing solely on the cost of snakeskin boots is not effective."

Do not use process improvement solely to achieve cost reduction. Cost is just one factor in the equation, although it is important. Do not be so focused on cost that you overlook opportunities to add customer value. Remember costs result from doing things that benefit the customer.

"How many stripes does that snake have?"

Management can become too fascinated with statistical measures to the detriment of the actual process, not to mention the customer. Management has to understand that better quality does not come merely through the use of more sophisticated statistics. It is also about the colours of the snake's stripes.

"Finding the snake's lair is a serious job."

Process improvement can also fail if teams do not care about root cause analysis. The natural tendency is for people to jump from identifying a problem to finding a solution, without first addressing the root cause. You may kill one snake, but you are leaving the rest of them to appear again.

"I don't care about the snakes!"

A lack of top and middle management commitment will cause serious problems. Implementing a process improvement programme requires top management's support or you are doomed to fail.

"I'm blaming the other snake killers!"

Consultants can help to adapt process improvement methods. A greater danger is that the entire responsibility for the process improvement programme will be put on the consultants. Management must accept on-going involvement and do their share of the snake killing. Consultants can help to show the flashlight into the dark lair, but management has to walk into it.

"Be gentle on the snakes and tell them to leave the paradise."

Do not neglect the so-called "soft skills" of communication and human interaction. Great statistical measurements will not do you much good if people lack meeting skills, cannot communicate, and are not able to work together. Put strong emphasis on customer communications.

"Indifferent snakes do harm."

Employees need training that creates true behavioural change, not programmes that just hand out information. Information and skills are worthless without being put into practice.

"Holding snake from the tail will cause problems."

Poor quantity and/or quality of training will cause unhealthy working habits. A process improvement programme needs sufficient, appropriate resources, including training, so people learn to use new tools and methods properly—and this means everyone in the organisation.

Summary

As you can see, many kinds of snakes can live in process paradise. If any of them seem familiar to you, maybe you should spend a few minutes thinking about what you are going to do about it. Remember, it is not the thoughts, but the appropriate actions that you will take after thinking, which will bring the results to your garden.

Here are some reflective questions you can ask yourself to promote your thinking:

- What kind of problems have you had in your process initiatives?
    o Where do they initiate?
- Who is the most important stakeholder in your organisation?
- How is change embraced in your organisation?
    o Is change something that people are ok with or resist?
- What other goals do you have for process improvement initiatives besides cost reduction?
- When solving problems, do you find the root cause or mainly focus on removing effects?

Write down your own thoughts here:

WEEK 7: INGREDIENTS FOR PROCESS CULTURE THAT BRING THE RESULTS

Change culture is the driving force in process improvement initiatives. The culture must support the fundamental ideology behind the reason for an organisation to exist. And as we all know, every organisation exists to fulfil customers' needs and wants in one way or another. Process improvement requires the right kind of organisational culture to support it. Here are a few things that you can consider while building your organisation for better process improvement results.

Have genuine focus on the customer

The customer is everyone's business, no matter what function a person has in an organisation. Even people in "internal roles" should be doing something that enables others to serve customers. Always seek customer satisfaction and value through fulfilling their needs. Make sure your employees understand that customers will always want something, but even more important is to know what they need. Serve the cause, not the effect.

Your organisation needs a culture, where focus is on mastering processes from a customer-oriented perspective

Build a competitive advantage in delivering value to customers. People do what they are rewarded for, so make sure that you give out the goodies for the right reasons. You do not necessarily need to give bonuses, just pay the appropriate salary for delivering successful customer outcomes.

Have data- and fact-driven management

Clarity key measures for gauging business performance, gather the necessary data and analyse it using key variables. You get what you measure. Build your balanced scorecard from a customer-oriented perspective and make sure everyone sees and understands those results. With every KPI, ask: "How does this help my customer to succeed?" That will help you to think about your organisation's internal matters from a customer-oriented perspective. If something does not contribute to providing great customer experiences, get rid of them.

Create silo-free collaboration culture

Break down organisational barriers to improve teamwork throughout the organisation. It might be best to have truly process-oriented structure in your organisation, so that everyone gets what he or she needs to do provide profitable customer experiences. Do not support old-fashioned departmental silos that prevent people from collaborating.

Require proactive management

Set goals for providing customer experiences, review them frequently, establish clear priorities and focus on problem prevention rather than resolutions after the fact. Have your people anticipate problems before they even occur. The cost of fixing a cause of a problem is lower the earlier it is detected.

Support a drive for perfection, combined with a tolerance for failure

You must be willing to try new ideas and approaches that have some risk of failure in order to make changes which can lead to perfection. Just make sure that you learn from the mistakes that you will make on the way. If you cannot extract a teaching from a failure, you better stop trying. No failure is a failure if you learn something from it; it is just a lesson of how not to do something (as Edison concluded while trying to create a light bulb).

Summary

The six things mentioned in this chapter are fairly big issues to handle, but they are the very important for the successful process improvement initiatives. Which one of these cultural factors is the strongest in your organisation? And which one is the weakest? Spend a few minutes evaluating what you can do to strengthen the weak factors and make an action plan to do it.

Here are some reflective questions you can ask yourself to promote your thinking:
- Have you evaluated your customers' needs to understand them really well?
   o Do you purposefully deliver against those needs?
- Do you reward people in your organisation for creating successful customer outcomes?
- Is working in departmental silos preventing people from being more productive?

Write down your own thoughts here:

WEEK 8: PROCESS PERSPECTIVE ON THE BLUE OCEAN STRATEGY

The Blue Ocean strategy is highly related to process innovation. The idea of this strategy is to build new businesses where none existed before. So-called Blue Ocean industries are more profitable than traditional business fields with head-to-head competitors. In Blue Ocean strategy, you must offer your customers a value innovation (i.e. tangible product or service advancements) accompanied by demonstrable savings. To be able to do that, you have to look at your process innovation from a new perspective. Let's revisit the six steps of Blue Ocean strategy from a process point of view.

Reconstruct market boundaries

In Blue Ocean strategy you must re-evaluate the premises that form your industry's assumptions and shape your company's business model. The easiest way to do that is to think: where does the process start for your customers and where does it really end? That does not only lead to an expanded value chain, but also into completely new markets. Think about, for example, Ryanair, which is not only flying people, but also providing the whole holiday experience with accommodation and car rentals included. The holiday does not start and end for people when they fly (that is how traditional airlines used to think).

Focus on the big picture

Keep your eye on the overall view and don't get lost in the statistics. Many business strategists get lost in the data jungle, so they often miss where they, and their competition, are headed. You have to think about what your customers really need from you and how your organisation can provide them with successful outcomes. Ask yourself every week: what do we have in our business processes that customers are not benefiting from?

Reach beyond the existing demand

Businesses naturally focus on current customers, a process that invariably leads to greater market segmentation analysis. However, real growth lies beyond existing demand. To get to the open water, focus on potential future customers. Apple were not satisfied with just creating new versions of the iPhone; they reinvented how people work with portable devices by introducing the iPad. That created new horizons beyond the traditional smartphone market.

Get the strategic sequence right

Execute your strategy sequentially to achieve your value innovation. To be compelling, the technology must provide convenience, safety and entertainment. It has to make your customer's life easier, simpler and more successful. Plan the experience you want buyers to have at all stages. Assess your service's or product's usefulness, ease, handiness, safety, entertainment value, and environmental friendliness, in light of how each factor affects the customer upon buying it, bringing it home, using it, adding to it, keeping it working and eventually, disposing of it. Remember that the customer experience is the process.

Overcome key organisational hurdles

Successful execution demands that your organisation must resolve internal departmental differences. If you are still working in silos, try to create process bridges over them so that in the eyes of the customer you offer products and services as one, solid company. Do not let your internal politics, bureaucracy, silos or other things get in the way of you providing the perfect customer experience every time.

Build execution into strategy

Reduce your management risk by incorporating Blue Ocean implementation into your organisation's on-going processes. Make providing great customer experiences your main business. Teach people to think outside of the box at all times and make sure that they are empowered to improve the processes. Make problem solving a team effort that everyone wants to participate in. If you do not build a culture of executing great customer experiences into your organisation's strategy, people will never do it. You can see that, for example, from Zappos who are not just selling shoes, but are providing exceptional customer experiences that exceed expectations.

Summary

To succeed in Blue Ocean strategy, a value innovation must demonstrate actual savings and an appreciable benefit that a customer can use immediately. Your organisation has to be able to fulfil the needs of your customers consistently all the time. The idea of Blue Ocean strategy is to build new businesses where none existed before and the best way for you to do that is to start thinking about your processes from a customer perspective.

Here are some reflective questions you can ask yourself to promote your thinking:

- Are your organisation's market boundaries clear to you?
- Do you understand where your customer's market boundaries are?
- Are you playing with numbers or seeing the big picture?
- Do you understand where demand for services and products in your target customer groups come from?
- Are you able to work together as a team towards a common goal or do internal hurdles slow you down?
- Is providing exceptional customer experiences built into your organisation's strategy?

Write down your own thoughts here:

WEEK 9: HOW TO REWARD PEOPLE FOR THE RIGHT THINGS IN BPM?

Do you have a reward model in your organisation? Have you ever thought about who has designed it and for what purpose? Sometimes Human Resources design the reward model to keep people committed to the organisation. In some organisations, management designs the reward model to keep people motivated to work. The finance department may reward people based on financial numbers like growth in turnover and profit, and in some cases that is not a bad idea to share the wealth that the organisation receives. The problem in this, however, is that people may not know what exactly they are supposed to do in order to raise those numbers. How many times have people been told to get 20% more revenue this year and they are working on an assembly line? It is really hard to see a connection between the two, even though it does exist.

Business Process Management (BPM) is about managing everything that is done in an organisation to provide successful customer outcomes. Furthermore, people do what they are paid or rewarded for. Thus, organisations should combine the two things together and get the benefits of one serving the other. According to BPM research, it is very important that a reward model adjusts to business needs and the processes fulfilling them. One study has shown that about 80% of organisations in Finland have some kind of reward model. The question is, how many of those organisations have designed the reward system to support proper Business Process Management?

If you have a reward model in your organisation, take a few minutes to evaluate how many of the items that it has for evaluation actually helps your customer to succeed? How many of them support you in improving business processes so that they will produce better results? I would bet that the answer is not many. What *should* those reward models be based on then? I will discuss a few thoughts on that in the following paragraphs.

A reward model should be adjusted based on process changes

If you do not change the reward model when you change business processes, people are going to keep on doing what they are used to. The answer to this is not to have high-level economic measurements for rewarding, because as I mentioned earlier, people may not know what to do. The reward model should reflect the things that will motivate people to act accordingly to result in successful customer outcomes. The model will have to reflect the business that you are in. For consultants you can have more outcome-oriented measurements while for people working in manufacturing lines you need more accurate ones. The difference to traditional thinking is that the reward model is based on outcomes as well as the flexibility.

A reward model should be based on providing successful customer outcomes

As we all know, customers pay for those rewards. Is it not then fair to reward for results that they benefit from? Rewarding people for growth in turnover will not help employees to think about the customers. You get what you reward for and you reward for what you get. Providing successful customer outcomes through well-designed business processes is a good reason to reward people. This requires changing the old mindset of setting economical goals and controlling people with them. You will receive the economic outcomes if your people are doing the right things.

Summary

In summary, my recommendation is to abandon the old ways of thinking about the reward models from the organisation's internal perspective. Successful companies in the twenty-first century design their reward models to support the successful customer outcomes produced through well thought-out business processes.

Here are some reflective questions you can ask yourself to promote your thinking:
- Do you have a reward model in your organisation?
  - o Is it measuring the right things, i.e. creating successful customer outcomes?
- How do you perceive that your HR department supports customer work?
- What is the role of HR in your organisation?
  - o How does that help to create value to customers in a profitable way?
- How is your reward model aligned to produce income?

Write down your own thoughts here:

WEEK 10: HOW TO LAUNCH A BPM PROGRAMME SUCCESSFULLY?

Any process development programme is a phased programme. The first important phase is the launch. You need a plan which includes a description from the organisation regarding how it will roll out the Business Process Management (BPM) initiative, select processes for development and train people to lead the actual implementation. Planning for successful BPM deployment should include, but is not limited to, the following steps.

Choose a suitable BPM method

Not every process development method is suitable for every organisation; you should make sure that you pick the one that helps your organisation and then stick with it for long enough to get the benefits. If you have experienced help in BPM, you can combine the best aspects of different methods and make your own mix that best serves your needs. None of the existing BPM methods are the silver bullet.

Have executive workshops to train top-level people for BPM

It is very important to have top management on board all the time. They should understand why BPM is important and how it can help to develop strategy further. Business processes are a way of implementing customer strategy and top-level people can be helped to understand that by providing workshops designed for their needs.

Training people is important

If you are in the service business, then train people in Customer Experience Management (CEM). If you manufacture something, look into Lean or Six Sigma and train enough champions, master black belts and such. BPM is not any one method, it contains several methods, so train your people to whatever process method you decide to use. Ensure everybody in your organisation at least understands the basics.

Create a clear statement of goals and a strategy for achieving them

There is no point proceeding with BPM unless you have a goal to achieve. And since everything that is done in an organisation is BPM, no organisation can achieve success without a clear purpose. Keep your goals clear and the strategy for achieving them even clearer. Make sure that each business development you do contributes to those goals. Everyone in your organisation should understand the common goals and which strategy is being implemented to achieve them.

Measure process performance and schedule them for review

You get what you measure, so make sure that you measure the outcomes that you want to receive. Much of the time, organisations have KPIs that are internally focused and do not measure the right things. Once you have measured the right things, you need to follow how those results develop. You should have scheduled reviews for process performance to learn what you can do better and how.

Make a communications plan

Nowadays, all work requires communication and cooperation. You need to have a plan for how you are going to communicate the business development to different stakeholders. Evaluate what information is important to whom and how to share it. If you manage to communicate this well, other problems will be able to solve themselves. By the same token, if you handle communications poorly, you are likely to experience problems that did not exist before.

Create a system for identifying and prioritising projects

You need to identify what process improvement projects are needed and then prioritise them. Here, the Pareto rule applies; you will get 80% of process improvement benefits from 20% of processes. The best way to optimise processes is to get rid of processes that do not contribute to successful customer outcomes and improve the rest.

Have a system for monitoring and auditing the progress of BPM projects

It is important that you not only monitor processes, but also develop them. Make sure that your BPM projects stay on the right track. You can also have internal and external auditions for BPM projects to maintain the quality.

Plan for rewards, incentives and recognition

Only pay for things that contribute to creating successful customer outcomes. Reward for useful innovations, give incentives for excellent work and give recognition for improving business processes. People do what they are paid for, so make sure that you pay for the things that help the organisation to provide better customer experiences. Even little details matter, so do not overlook them; if they matter to the customer, they should matter to you. Create a culture of positive change into your organisation.

Summary

After a successful launch phase, it is time to move on to the management phase. It is important not to stay in one place, but to develop business processes all the time as customer expectations evolve. BPM is not a one-shot project; it needs to be an iterative on-going process. When you come up with really good ways to do things, your competitors will subsequently mimic it and therefore you need to be ready to take the next step forward.

Here are some reflective questions you can ask yourself to promote your thinking:

- Do you have a standardised method for process improvement in use?
- Does top management recognise that improving processes is critical to business success?
- Have you trained most of your employees in the chosen BPM method?
- Do you have clear goals for process improvement initiatives?
- Do you measure the outcomes rather than activities?
- Have you done a stakeholder communication plan (e.g. RACI)?
- Do you monitor and control developing processes?

Write down your own thoughts here:

WEEK 11: HOW TO BUILD CUSTOMER SATISFACTION INTO BUSINESS PROCESSES?

Managing customer expectations and providing great customer service is more important today than ever. To achieve this, you should build customer satisfaction into business processes, which is everything that the organisation does. Traditionally, organisations measure customer satisfaction once each year, long after the service has been provided. Some organisations may measure customer satisfaction after the service, project or product has been delivered and then take corrective actions. The problem with that kind of approach is that they are reactive, not proactive ways to respond to customer satisfaction. If you build customer satisfaction into business processes, you do not have to read the negative feedback about your actions after it is too late. Here are some ideas of how to build customer satisfaction into your business processes.

"KYSS – keep your systems simple."

Do not track everything, just what you need. Focus on major attributes that contribute to successful customer outcomes. To keep on top of the details about your customers, develop a tracking system listing their traits and main preferences. Update it after each interaction to keep it fresh. Customers will be happier if your employees do not need to take a long time to browse through complex systems to serve them.

"If it is important to your customer, it belongs in your tracking system."

Record service preferences and personal data, which help you to serve them better. Include pertinent information on any previous missteps on your organisation's part concerning this customer and make sure that those problems will not rise again. Customers will remember the mistakes that you have made and so should you. Do not record the mistakes to punish your employees, but to learn and improve.

"The information you gather needs to be available in real time."

Make sure all front-line employees have immediate access to the tracking system. You should not ask the customers to tell you something that you should already know. If the customer contact comes through e-mail, connect that with your CRM. If you receive a phone call, identify the customer by their phone number. If they walk into your store, remember them if you can, and if you can't, then have customer loyalty system that identifies the customer.

"Because customer preferences change, assumptions are dangerous."

Just because a customer once ordered coffee after dinner does not mean that customer will always want coffee after dinner. Know your customers' preferences, but do not get locked down because of them. You can ask them, for example, "would you like to have some coffee after your dinner?". Do not be afraid to bring more value, for example by asking if they would like to have some Costa Rican coffee that you imported yourself last week.

"Customers' moods change, so you need to track them."

Have your people track customers' moods and make it their business to lift their spirits up. If people feel better after they leave your business than before they came in, then you have succeeded. This feeling will make them come back and your employees will feel better about themselves, as they could make someone's day better. It will also give a positive kick to revenues. Be proactive, not reactive.

"Do not dampen the customer's experience with an impersonal delivery."

People like to be treated as individuals. Make every customer count and do not overlook one for another. It is true that some customers are more valuable to the organisation than others, but you should never show that to your customers. For example, use the customer's name on a liberal basis, always with a sincere, engaged manner. Teach everyone in your organisation good manners: to say hello and goodbye, thank you and other polite ways of working. Watch out for the caveat that your employees may look false when being polite if they do not want to be polite (you need to create a personal culture to serve customers in your organisation).

"Use technology to ask for customer's information sparingly."

Ask only what you need to know to serve them better and they will happily share this information. Employ your database information discreetly. Do not sound like Big Brother is watching them. You do not want customers to think you spy on them. Additionally, state clearly the purpose that the information is being gathered for. After you have the information, use it! Too many organisations collect information just for the sake of it and they do not use it intelligently to serve the customer.

Summary

To provide exceptional service, employees must think like your customers. Have your people eat in your restaurant or shop at your store. Let your employees use your services so that they can see how they work. The old methods of measuring customer satisfaction do not serve you anymore and the reason is that you need to be proactive, not reactive. That requires you to build customer satisfaction as part of your business processes. Your employees need to know what may go wrong before it happens, so that they can prevent customers from suffering from it. When you manage to do that, you will not have to send them an annual customer satisfaction survey and take corrective actions long after customers have already dealt with the consequences.

Here are some reflective questions you can ask yourself to promote your thinking:

- Do you measure customer satisfaction once per year or in real time? How would changing that benefit you?
- Are you using Net Promoter Score or a similar technique to measure the recommendation rate?
- How well connected are people in your organisation to customers' moods?
- Does your organisation treat customers as individuals? How would doing that benefit you?
- Are your customer feedback surveys exhaustive? How could you increase the response rate?
- Are you more reactive or proactive when it comes to customer satisfaction? How would becoming more proactive benefit you?

Write down your own thoughts here:

WEEK 12: WHAT COULD HELP TO MAKE CHANGE MORE SUSTAINABLE?

Change is constant; in fact, the only thing that does not change is change. That may be one reason why so many organisations are looking for ways to make change sustainable and easier to execute. And as you might have already guessed, there is no silver bullet solution available out there. Here are some thoughts that might help you to make change more sustainable.

Taking your own medicine

How many factories do you know who send their wastewater upstream of their water intake? It is easy to bring the fresh water from upstream and put your waste water downstream without suffering from the effects. Or using another analogy, how many IT companies do you know who use their own software themselves? Do you actually use and try out the services and products that you offer to your customers? Are there some annoying small problems in your services that you are already so used to getting around? Do you think your customer will take that trouble to learn to get around the bugs that your products have?

Resolutions

It is quite common to make New Year's resolutions. Perhaps you made some last year? How many resolutions are already forgotten about? Were you ever intent on achieving those resolutions or was it just something you do traditionally on New Year's Eve? Do you think the same way about the decisions you make in your organisation? Do you make them to stick to and do whatever it takes to achieve them, or are they just nice words on a memo?

Short-term thinking

It is easy to see a pattern of short-term solutions everywhere. For example, in America's recent housing boom they reached a point where families could no longer afford housing. The short-term solution was to engineer suicide financing: loans that gave the appearance that the system was still functioning normally. Consequently, it self-destructed and initiated a huge decline in the economy. If you happen to work in a software company, then you are even more familiar with this kind of duct tape fix. You fix a bug just to cover your tracks and hope that it will be someone else's job to fix the actual cause…and the customers keep on paying.

Big-picture thinking

In the early twentieth century, Henry Ford wanted to expand the market for his cars. His approach was to make his workers more productive through better-designed processes. He could then pay them better, which he did—instituting an unheard-of $5 a day minimum wage at his factories in 1914, thereby doubling the wages of many of his workers. This then led to a larger market for his cars, as many workers were now able to afford cars for the first time. The point here is that Mr. Ford developed a sustainable solution that lasted for years. Thinking about the big picture will bring you better things in the long run.

Incentives

You need motivation to stick with the plan or even better inspiration to achieve continuous improvement. People need to have a *"Why stop here?"* attitude. Organisations need a leadership that allows failure and learns from those failures (that is how you accumulate experience). Change can only happen or become sustainable if there is a better choice or if the current state is painful enough. Otherwise, people will just stick to whatever they have. You need to analyse the thought and decision patterns of the group involved in the change and accommodate the change process to their needs.

Make it stick

How does all of this tie into Business Process Management? We have heard the complaints and stories of short-term gains from exciting initiatives such as SCOR, Six Sigma and Lean, which come with cynicism about how long the change lasts and what it really did for the bottom line in the long run. So, how can we make sustainable change in organisations?

- *Customer supported.* The most important of all and the result of doing the other things well. The customer is the reason for your organisation to exist.
- *Easy.* Sticky change is not too difficult to adopt and does not require excessive effort.
- *Executive supported.* Anything that is going to last has to be supported at a high level: the C-level.
- *Systematic.* Make business process improvement part of everyday business.
- *Customer supported.* The most important of all and the result of doing the other things well. The customer is the reason for your organisation to exist.

- *Cultural.* The things that define us as an organisation get more of our efforts. Make change part of your organisational culture.
- *Rewarding.* People do what they are rewarded for (money, fame, thanks, and so on).

Summary

The recipe for making change more sustainable is not an easy one, but nevertheless, it is very important. I suggest that we should all take our own medicine. That will help us to move from short-term thinking to long-term thinking, which will bring benefits. Sustain the change through making sensible resolutions and sticking to them. Follow the plan carefully until you change it; plans are made to be changed. When you design the change, try to see the big picture of change so that you will be able to understand how it will affect different aspects of your organisation.

Here are some reflective questions you can ask yourself to promote your thinking:
- Are you taking your own medicine?
    o If yes, how does it taste?
    o If not, why are you not taking it?
- Do you go after the long-term benefits or do you use a short cut?
- How do you reward your people?
- Are you rewarding for the right things?
- What do people in your organisation say when they hear the word 'change'?
- Are you able to see the big picture regardless of details?
- Are you offering people appealing enough options when introducing change?
- Do your people know that the customer is the reason for your organisation to exist?

Write down your own thoughts here:

WEEK 13: WHAT IS IMPORTANT IN THE INNOVATION MANAGEMENT PROCESS?

The innovation management process has become an important part of the operation of many businesses as the recognition of the importance of initiatives toward innovation has become much more common. That said, while many companies do attempt to have a solid approach to creativity and innovation, all too few actually focus on it as a single function. Instead, they seem to hold many separate activities in isolation—such as brainstorming sessions, pilot projects and campaigns, and vague communication with the market, and simply hope that it will come together in the end. While this has worked for some in the past, it is far from the ideal way of performing this important task. Instead, the best way to accomplish this is to have a set of innovation activities, which integrates the activity into the regular cycle of your business. The list below shows the phases in the innovation management process, which will help your organisation to put it all together as one process.

Setting the goals for the innovation process

An innovation always begins with a goal in mind. It is often based on finding a solution to a problem. Once you have this goal, it should be discussed among all members of the problem-solving team. This team may consist of you and another person, a group of people, or may even be all of your organisation's employees. It may even involve others such as your customers (who can provide suggestions and feedback based on their own experience with your product or service) or other stakeholders in the business. When you establish the team for this process, make sure that you have someone representing all the parts of the process from start to finish.

Cooperation

The innovation team should work together so that instead of trying to come up with an idea separately, they can bounce ideas off one another and create a collaborative solution. This can include the use of on-line tools, attendance of events such as trade shows that can be inspiring and informative, or simply consist of brainstorming sessions. You might consider having a trained business coach to facilitate the discussions.

Combination of ideas

Once the ideas are in, choose the best ones and then consider whether they can be combined to create an even greater idea. Often, strong ideas will be complementary to one another and will merge well to create an even better result. As you know, a whole result can be bigger than the combination of its individual parts. For this to work well, you need representatives of all parties involved in the process, because they will almost certainly have ideas that people from other departments could not come up with. A business coach may be useful here for making sure that all the angles of innovative aspect are covered.

Evaluation of innovation

This is an important and yet all too frequently overlooked aspect of the innovation management process. When the best ideas have been combined, fine-tuned, and polished, it is time to subject them to an evaluation based on peer reviews. This helps to ensure that any ideas that have a promising veneer but that are poorly thought-out will be identified before resources, funding and time have been poured into them. It also helps to select the ideas with the greatest potential from among several that appear equally capable of being successful. It is cheap to change your innovation at this stage compared to the cost at later stages. Each step you take forward will cost you more.

Testing the ideas

Once the ideas with the greatest potential have been identified, they can be tested so that they can be developed. One of the most common means of testing a product or service idea is to create a prototype or test group. This allows the team, as well as the customers and investors, to have a better look at how the product will function and what changes can be made to it before release. Make sure that the product or service not only raises interest but is also able to generate orders. If people say that they are interested in it, then ask them if they wish to put an order in straight away.

Execution of innovation implementation

The ideas that survive the testing process can be further developed and altered until they are ready to be executed as a part of the business offerings. The execution of implementation is a step that is unique to your business and, unless your new product causes you to have to drastically alter the typical way that your go-to-market strategy functions, then this part of the innovation management process should be relatively commonplace in your organisation. It should be easier for you to move from testing to execution if you were able to generate orders in the testing phase.

Assessment of innovation lifecycle

After the execution of an idea, its implementation needs to be carefully monitored and assessed in terms of a number of milestones that should be set. Should a milestone not be reached, then changes will need to be made or the idea will need to be shut down. Remember to always keep your customers in your mind here, as well as in the execution phase, and design your measuring systems so that they measure added value for the customer (you get what you measure and customers determine your value based on that).

The next step in the process is simply to start again, always finding new needs, inspiration, solutions and taking them through the cycle until they can be offered by your company.

Summary

When you start innovating processes, it is very important to start with the question, why? What is it that you want to achieve? Answering those questions will shape the process you want to use to manage innovation. Involve enough people during the planning of the innovation process, because a collective mind is usually more innovative than a single mind. Having people from different departments also helps to create cross-functional innovation and to decrease change resistance.

Here are some reflective questions that you can use to evaluate the innovation management process in your organisation:
- Do you have a clearly defined innovation management process?
    - If yes, is it effective?
    - If no, how do you see that clearly defined innovation management process helping your organisation to achieve goals better?
- Are all the people in your organisation working together towards great innovations or do they do things on their own?
- Do you always properly evaluate and test your innovations before taking them to market?
- Do you measure execution of the provision of services or products from the customer's perspective?

Write down your own thoughts here:

WEEK 14: HOW CAN BUSINESS COACHING HELP YOU REACH SPECIFIC GOALS?

"Business coaching has that unique factor which only a business coach can provide...accountability."
– Chris Rugh, 2011.

Do you recall the popular reality television show called *'The Biggest Loser'*? It is the one where overweight people try to lose their weight with a coach. The reason that these programmes get better results than just trying to lose weight on your own is accountability. The thought of having another person weigh you and see that you are overweight or obese is an incentive for weight loss in itself. Today, contestants on *'The Biggest Loser'* know that not only is their coach watching their progress, but so is the rest of the nation.

Business coaching is successful for entrepreneurs because the pressure of accountability works. The very reason business coaching works is because it is based on that same accountability factor. If another person is there to walk alongside us and monitor our progress and to help us when we get stuck or reach a plateau, we are more likely to succeed in our endeavours. Otherwise, we explain and rationalise what we are doing, and before we know it, our old habits are back.

Studies show that adults do not like change. Why not? We are creatures of habit. We get into a routine and we stick with it, even if we know that it is unhealthy, dangerous, or not in our best interests. Studies also show that it takes 28 days to make something a habit. So, whether you are trying to lose weight or reach a specific business or personal goal, the most crucial time is the first 28 days you are trying to implement it. Typically, if you give up within the first 28 days, you lose.

Business coaching can help you reach that specific goal, because the business coach knows that change is hard, and that reaching a specific goal requires a plan and active steps towards it. The business coach also knows how to hold you accountable for reaching your goals. Let's say you have a goal 'to work smarter, not harder' (something I do myself). How do you go about this with a business coach?

First, the business coach helps you to articulate and give a 'vision' of what working 'smarter' means in relation to your business. You do the work and the business coach helps you to find the ideas within you.

Second, once you know what "working smarter" means in your business setting, then the business coach can help you to clearly define the goals you want to set to accomplish your vision of working smarter, not harder. These goals need to be SMART (specific, measurable, achievable, realistic and timed).

Third, the business coach helps you to write out a series of action steps to help you to logically map out how to get from point A to point B to realise your goals. Big goals take small steps to achieve. And when those steps are something that really contribute towards your goal, you like to do them.

Fourth, and most important, the business coach then gets in the trenches with you to hold you accountable. They check in with you to monitor your progress as agreed with you. They know when to cheer you through your successes, and they know when and how to encourage you to move forward. It is this accountability factor, which cannot be undervalued.

Think about it. If we were all self-starters and disciplined, we would not need coaching: but most people are not. They need that outside perspective or person who can monitor their ability to 'change' or take on something new. They need someone to challenge them to succeed. According to some studies, business coaching is the most effective way of training employees into better results (much more effective than, for example, in-class training, because it is personal and targeted to meet your needs).

Before you know it, this year will be in your rear-view mirror and you will be motoring through next one. Make it a priority to invest in yourself and your business's success by hiring a business coach to help you identify and reach the goals, which are the most significant to your success for the upcoming year. You'll be glad that you implemented life business coaching into your company's framework.

Summary

A business coach can help you to reach specific goals better than you can reach them alone. The reason is that a coach helps you to define your goals better. Once you have done that you establish accountability for yourself, which the coach can support with follow-up actions. Too often we think about doing something, but never actually get around to doing it. Therefore, sustainable change comes from instilling new habits. That is something that a business coach can help you with.

Here are some reflective questions you can ask yourself to promote your thinking:
- Do you have something that you have always desired to do, but for one reason or another never got around to doing?
- What is stopping you from doing these things that you aspire to?
- How often do you make your goals and aspirations SMART? How could doing that help you to reach your goals?

- Do you regularly evaluate where you are and where you want to be in your life?

Write down your own thoughts here:

WEEK 15: SUCCEED WITH PERSONAL LEADERSHIP

The world is full of recipes for success, but too often we forget that success comes from within ourselves through the work what we do. I would even claim that success is mainly about attitude. When you have the right attitude, you focus on the right things, you overcome obstacles, you feel better and you work more efficiently. I am sure you know what happens if you have a bad attitude: nothing seems to work. Here are some questions for you to ask to become more successful through your own attitude towards other people and life. Even though you may not have an answer to every one of them, thinking about these matters will begin to take you towards your personal success.

Am I sure that those that I love feel loved by me?

Love is the all-healing force of the world. Too many couples go days, weeks or even months without showing each other their love. Everyone wants to be loved, but even more everyone wants to love. Any bad day will become better when you love someone and show it. Do not limit your love just to your spouse; tell your parents, best friends or any other people that you are close to that you love them and see the difference in your personal success.

Do I feel grateful every day for having whatever I have or get today?

Every day when I go to bed I list at least three things that I am thankful for. It really lifts your spirits to be grateful for what you have or you got that day. And do not limit it to that; be thankful for what you are going to get. Try it out for one week and see how it changes your thinking. When you face hard times, it is much easier when you are thankful for other things that you already have. Being thankful for something that you have not got yet will make you more determined to get it.

Have I done my best to avoid unkind acts and words?

Think positively. There is nothing to gain by vengeful actions, saying unpleasant things, or even thinking ungracious thoughts. You are judged by what you do, so if you commit unkind acts, people will judge you negatively. So, do yourself a favour and avoid all negative acts, words and thoughts. It will promote your personal success if you are the person who everyone wants to be with.

What can I do today to make the world better place?

All of us can do something to make this world a better place for everyone, every day. What have you done or what are you going to do today? As you well know, what goes around comes around.

Have I helped anyone less fortunate?

You are reading this, so you are certainly doing better than many other people in this world (many of them cannot read, do not have access to the Internet, etc.), so what can you do to help less fortunate people? Giving is the start of the receiving process.

Have I completed and reviewed my personal success plan?

Better tomorrow is earned today. Have you done and reviewed a good, sound personal success plan for a better future? You have very limited time in your life, so you better use it wisely. Have you written a personal mission statement? Have you set goals for this and next year? Have you identified your roles in your life? And did you write all that down and review it regularly so that you stay on track?

What worthwhile thing have I yet to accomplish?

What is your dream? Are you working towards it? Did you know that the only difference between a dream and a goal is that you are working towards it? Is there something out there that you really want to accomplish? Have you done a roadmap and are you walking along it? Many dreams can come true if you just work persistently towards them.

What wonderful memories do I have?

If you want to dwell on the past, you should dwell only on good memories. Get rid of bad memories by writing them down, learning whatever you can from them and then forgetting them. Enjoy the feeling of good memories and make bad memories tools for learning and get over them. Only good memories are of value to you (bad memories have value in teachings, but not in the memories themselves).

Does my integrity hold as well in public as in private?

Are you living a double life? If yes, then stop. The reason is that if you live your life by any rules other than your internal ones, you will have conflicts and lose energy in thinking about what you should do in each situation. Establish ground rules that you can live by in every situation. And review those rules when necessary. Deny those activities that do not suit your integrity and go fully with the ones that fit well with your inner peace.

Summary

Each of these questions is a big one and you can easily find many books to help you on your journey. The only thing you need to bear in mind is what you really want to achieve and keep on working towards it and one day you will succeed.

Here are some reflective questions you can ask yourself to promote your thinking:

- Am I sure that those I love feel loved by me?
- Do I feel grateful every day for having whatever I have or get today?
- Have I done my best to avoid unkind acts and words?
- What can I do today to make the world a better place?
- Have I helped anyone less fortunate?
- Have I done and reviewed my personal success plan?
- What worthwhile thing have I yet to accomplish?
- What wonderful memories do I have?
- Does my integrity hold as well in public as in private?

Write down your own thoughts here:

WEEK 16: DO YOU WANT TO HAVE FEWER INCIDENTS OF SICK LEAVE IN YOUR ORGANISATION?

Did you know that good leadership causes your employees to take less sick leave? In Finland, up to 220 million Euro are lost annually due to unfinished work owing to sick leave. That contributes to up to 14% of each person's salary. For each individual's work every year, companies pay up to 5,300 Euro in expenses related to this. Here are some tips on how you can start using good leadership to have fewer incidents of sick leave in your organisation.

It is all about top management commitment

You cannot simply outsource healthcare of employees to healthcare professionals. Leaders have the responsibility of making sure that everyone is capable of completing their work. Healthcare professionals are not able to affect the work conditions at the work place directly in the same way as leaders can.

Dig a little deeper

Find out where all the sick leave expenses come from in your company. What causes them? As you well know, repairing the effect is not useful in comparison to repairing the cause. What kind of sick leave is the most common? In which departments? What causes this? What can you do about it?

Improve working conditions

Set goals to reduce sick leave in your organisation by improving working conditions. You can take several steps to get rid of the causes of sick leave in your organisation. Maybe you need to adjust working times? Or improve healthcare? Or offer new incentives? Just be careful that you do not build systems where people are rewarded for not caring about their health. That will cause big problems in the long run.

Network and discuss with relevant healthcare partners

Benefit from networking. Ask your health insurance company to help you. Find out about other professionals that improve, for example, ergonomics, air conditioning, workload, etc. Have discussions about healthcare. Talk to your employees and create an environment where people want to take care of themselves. Offer healthy food and snacks, make sure people have breaks and remember to stretch. The right food gives people energy, the right drinks keep them refreshed, and breaks activate their brains.

Ask for quality

Ask for good quality healthcare. I bet you have sometimes had such bad flu that you just could not work, but you got over it with good medication and care. In the same way, ask for good quality healthcare for your employees. Make sure they will receive suitable doctors and medication. In the long run, that will save you more money than it costs.

Train and prevent

Train managers and leaders about healthcare. Make sure that they understand that the health of their subordinates is their responsibility. If those managers are bad and employees are burdened by his leadership style, train them or replace them.

Take preventative measures. Offer people the chance to have health checkups and physical examinations. Offer team sports (that will improve both employees' health and team spirit). Organise some playful sport competitions (for example, who can cycle the most this summer? Who can run the most this summer? Who can improve their push-ups most in next two months?).

Summary

You can start saving money by evaluating ways to have less incidents of sick leave in your organisation.

Here are some reflective questions you can ask yourself to promote your thinking:
- Do your managers and leaders care about their subordinates' health?
- Do you actually know how much sick leave costs you every year?
- Have you analysed and made plans to reduce sick leave in your company?
- Do you take preventative measures to promote your employees' health?

Write down your own thoughts here:

WEEK 17: HOW TO MOTIVATE EMPLOYEES BESIDES WITH MONEY?

It is always a big question for leaders—how can they motivate people in their organisation? Money only takes you so far and after that other means are necessary. Some research says that after people receive a certain amount of money, more money will not increase their happiness. Leaders can and have to motivate their employees with means other than money to get long-term results. This week gives some tips on how to motivate employees.

Get rid of the managers

Removing the project lead or supervisor and empowering your employees to work together as a team rather than everyone reporting to one individual can do wonders. What is even worse than letting your boss down? Letting your team down! Allowing people to work together as a team on an equal level with their co-workers will often produce better projects faster. Maybe you should give it a try ?

Make your ideas theirs

Do you like it when you are told what to do? Instead of telling people what you want done—"I would like you to do it this way"—ask them in a way that will make them feel like they came up with the idea: "Do you think it is a good idea if we do it this way?"

Do not criticise or correct

Nobody wants to hear that they did something wrong. If you are looking for a demotivator, this is it. Try an indirect approach to get people to improve, learn from their mistakes, and fix them. Ask, "Was that the best way to approach the problem? Why not? Have you got any ideas about what you could have done differently?" This way you are having a conversation and talking through solutions, not pointing the finger.

Be generous with praise

Everyone wants it and it is one of the easiest things to give. Praise from the boss goes a lot further than you might think. Praise every improvement that you see your team members make. Once you are comfortable delivering praise one-on-one to an employee, try praising them in front of others, because that will bring even more results.

Share the rewards and the pain

When your company does well, celebrate. This is the best time to let everyone know that you are thankful for their hard work. Go out of your way to show how far you will go when people help your company to succeed. Buy champagne, do something spectacular. If there are disappointments, share those too. If you expect high performance levels, your team deserves to know where the company stands. Be honest and transparent, but remember that no one wants to hear that they did something wrong.

Make everyone a leader

Highlight your top performers' strengths and let them know that because of their excellence, you want them to be an example for others. You'll set the bar high and they will be motivated to live up to their reputation as a leader. Take an employee to lunch once a week. Surprise them. Do not make an announcement that you are establishing a new policy. Literally walk up to one of your employees and invite them to lunch with you. It is an easy way to remind them that you notice and appreciate their work.

Summary

Money is a good motivator, but everyone has a threshold after which it ceases to continue to have the same effect. It is very beneficial to find "softer" ways to reward people besides money. Genuine appreciation and respect are free and highly regarded by the recipient, so use them to motivate employees.

Here are some reflective questions that you can use to evaluate how you could improve on motivating your employees without giving out money:
- Do you share all the successes and situations where improvement is needed with your employees?
- Do you give feedback in a constructive way, without criticism?
- Do you have shared leadership with everyone doing their share of the load?
- Do you give spontaneous acknowledgment to your employees?
- Who do you eat your lunches with? And your coffee breaks?
- Do you have useless managers?

Write down your own thoughts here:

WEEK 18: WHAT CAN YOU DO TO CREATE BETTER CUSTOMER EXPERIENCES?

Would you like to create better customer experience for your organisation's customers? Here are some ideas about what you could do to take your customers' experiences to the next level.

Make a connection with your customers

A personal connection with customers creates an emotional bond, regardless of the channel the customer is using. For example, many organisations have instructed their employees to greet customers within 15 seconds and engage those who would like to have a dialogue about their interests. But be careful not to fall into that classical dialogue trap: "Good day, sir! How may I help you?"... "Hi, no thanks, I am just looking around." How can you make your customers feel truly welcome?

Get rid of stupid rules

Get rid of any processes that hurt customers. "*Getting rid of one or more of these rules can quickly and cost-efficiently increase satisfaction*", is what the CEI professionals say. For example, by using the Customer Experience Innovation Method, hundreds of organisations have been able to get rid of useless rules that hurt the business.

Inject the unexpected into service or product

"*Adding some small cool things to give service a twist is a simple and inexpensive way to give your customer experience a positive vibe*", suggests the CEO of a retail company in Finland. She says that an imaginatively differentiated product or service can be an engaging element of the customer experience and can encourage recommendations. One hotel chain has a greeting card under each bed, which says: "Yes, we clean here, too!"

Use on-line communities for your benefit

You can get really good insight through on-line communities and forums. Your customers will 'Google you', so why don't you too? It is important to listen to customers' conversations within social media to gain a better understanding of customers' behaviours, needs and preferences.

Find passion internally

You should search your organisation internally for customer champions rather than only relying on outside experts. The best data and insights that you need to carry out customer experience activities are right within your own organisation. You should appoint a customer experience leader and designate him/her to form and lead a centralised customer experience team.

Reuse the buzz that customers are creating for you

Nowadays, many organisations are realising that when it comes to the Internet, social media and on-line technology, they should take an "*if you can't beat them, join them*" approach and go where customers already are. This way, customer discussions across multiple social networks are centralised in a single searchable space. In practice, this means that a comment or an article submitted by a customer on your Facebook page or Twitter feed can become available on your website and other places too.

Leverage analytics and reporting tools

Too many organisations have gathered a lot of information in their CRM systems without using them properly. A quick way to gain or maintain a strong lead in terms of customer experience is to use analytics and reporting tools to look at this information. For example, Best Buy used a reporting tool early on in the economic downturn to understand why although more customers were applying for financing for their purchases, there was also a drop in purchases costing more than $1,000.

Summary

Customers are the most valuable asset that your organisation will ever have. They are the ones keeping you in business. Based on over 10 years of research, it has been proven that revenues follow customer experience with a time lag. Therefore, you should really put some effort into evaluating how to improve the customer experience your organisation creates. Seek a connection with customers and make doing business with you easy. Since there are so many technological solutions nowadays, do not see them as the end, but rather as the means to create the real end, which is a great customer experience.

Here are some reflective questions you can use to think about how you could create a better customer experience:
- Do you connect with your customers in a genuine, meaningful way?

- Do you have rules or processes that you should get rid of?
- Do you evaluate your customer experience periodically?
- Do you have little extra things in your services or products that customer appreciate?
- Are people in your organisation passionate about promoting your organisation on-line?
- Are you reusing the good customer experiences that your customers share?
- Do you use your CRM and customer data efficiently?

Write down your own thoughts here:

WEEK 19: ARE YOU LOSING YOUR PRODUCTIVITY? HERE IS HOW TO GET IT BACK!

Do you need to improve productivity or are you losing your productivity? Personally, I sometimes feel like I get nothing done. At this point, it is time to stop and take a look at what you are doing. Here are some ideas that you can use to evaluate and find ways for recovering your productivity.

Stop multi-tasking

You seriously have to stop doing it. Changing from task to task quickly does not work. In fact, changing tasks more than 10 times in a day makes your brain malfunction. According to some claims, when you multi-task, your IQ drops by an average of 10 points.

Work backwards from goals to milestones to tasks

Writing "make sales worth £2 million this year" at the top of your to-do list is one great way to make sure you never get it done. Break down the work into smaller and smaller chunks until you have specific tasks that can be accomplished in a few hours or less: contact customer A, update price for product Z, etc. That is how you set goals and actually succeed in crossing them off your list sooner rather than later.

Be strict about eliminating distractions

Put a "do not disturb" sign up, lock your door, and turn off your phone, e-mail, and instant messaging. In fact, if you know you may sneak a peek at your e-mail, set it to off-line mode, or even turn off your Internet connection. Read e-mail only when you have planned to do so. Go to a quiet area and focus on completing the one task at hand.

Work to your own agenda

Don't let something else set your day. Most people go straight to their e-mails and start freaking out. You will end up with your inbox at zero, but accomplish nothing. After you wake up, drink water so you rehydrate, eat a good breakfast to replenish your glucose, then set prioritised goals for the rest of your day. Breakfast is the most important meal of the day, so do not skip it with just a cup of coffee. Embrace the coming day and while eating, think what you need to do today to feel happy and confident about that day.

Schedule your e-mail

Pick a maximum of two or three times during the day when you are going to check your e-mail. Checking your e-mail constantly throughout the day creates a lot of noise and kills your productivity. Start using the phone again and send a snail mail letter if the matter is not urgent (people actually get very little traditional mail nowadays).

Use the phone or meet face-to-face

E-mail is not meant for conversations. Do not reply more than twice to an e-mail. Pick up the phone instead. It really is worth it... You can get the matter settled with one phone call versus 10 e-mails and possible misunderstanding. Even better would be to go and meet the other person face-to-face. This way you are not restricted by the loss of information in communication (such as the body language).

Work in maximum of 90-minute intervals

Your brain uses up more glucose than any other bodily activity. Typically you will have spent most of it after 60–90 minutes (that's why you feel so burnt-out after particularly long meetings). So take a break: get up, go for a walk, have a snack, do something completely different to recharge.

Summary

As a summary, to improve your productivity: focus, focus, focus! And stop procrastinating and multi-tasking. If you are able to do these three things, you'll see an immediate increase in your personal productivity. Guaranteed!

Here are some reflective questions you can ask yourself to promote your thinking:
- Do I spend too much time on e-mail?
- Are you breaking up your goals into smaller tasks that are easier to accomplish?
- Do you reward yourself somehow after you have achieved a big goal?
- Do you work for excessively long periods? Are you having enough breaks?
- Do you consider your blood glucose levels and remember to have snacks?

Write down your own thoughts here:

WEEK 20: HOW CAN YOU GAIN MORE INFLUENCE?

You do not have to be a famous author, TV show host or politician to gain more influence. According to some research, you influence more than four people every day. If you want to become successful and positively affect other people, you must learn how to become a person of influence.

However, you need to bear in mind that you cannot become influential overnight. It takes you time and practise to build your influence around people. My mentor, John C. Maxwell, describes four different levels of influence:

- *Modelling.* People are always influenced by first impressions and what they hear from you affects their opinion from the beginning. You can then start working from that point towards increasing influence over time.

- *Motivating.* Your influence on others will increase as you connect with them emotionally and begin to build meaningful relationships. People will have to enjoy interacting with you and believe that they will benefit from that experience.

- *Mentoring.* When you are mentoring, you have decided to actively engage in others' lives and play an active role by aiding their professional and personal growth. That is different from coaching in which the coach has a less active role.

- *Multiplying.* Those people you have influenced will become role models to others. This level is difficult to reach and it will bring the biggest benefits for everyone.

When you start building your influence on others, you should start from building your integrity. You cannot get long-term benefits without being truthful, upright and moral. It will include admitting when you are wrong, putting others ahead of yourself, making decisions that may not be in your personal interest, and fulfilling promises that you have made. You have to make people trust you and you can only do that by becoming trustworthy. You have to build your inner core around integrity and then prepare yourself for situations where your core might be compromised. You can do that by deciding how you will react to a moral dilemma before it occurs.

You also need to show faith in people. People around you need good feedback and constructive suggestions. Show genuine concern towards people around you and help them to succeed. If you have employees, you need to make them feel important. Work through each person's strengths and give them opportunities to succeed. Limit your negative comments and give constructive feedback when you are alone. But remember to give praise in front of everyone!

When building influence, it is far more important to listen than to talk. Too many people are so intent on expressing their own thoughts that they overlook listening to others. Being a skilful listener is one of the keys to interpersonal relationships. Good listeners are patient, open and non-judgemental; they offer feedback wisely. So, pay close attention, maintain eye contact and note the body language of the other people. Your goal with others has to be to reach an understanding—that is to appreciate the other person's viewpoint without being judgmental.

Summary

Power is nothing; influence is everything. You can only force people so far, but you can inspire them through influential leadership to the end of the world (literally). The first thing you need to decide is what you want to be influential at. That will help you to focus your efforts on becoming influential on that matter. I have chosen to become influential in business processes and customer experience management and leadership. I am building my influence base on these three things. Building integrity is very important, but for some reason people seem to neglect that. Be who you are and people will follow you if they see something they want to follow. But if you are something else other than what you are, they will see through you and your influence will have no solid base.

You can use the following reflective questions to evaluate how you could gain more influence:

- Which level of influence are you at the moment?
- What should you do to get to the next level?
- Are you trustworthy?
- Do you have faith in other people or does everything always depend on you?
- Are you able to listen to others?

Write down your own thoughts here:

WEEK 21: WHY DO PEOPLE NEED TO BE LED?

There is so much talk about leadership that it feels like a good question to ask why do people need to be led at all? Why do we need leaders, managers and such? Shouldn't educated, capable people be able to cope without a supervisor?

Actually, leadership has become increasingly more important when the competition gets tougher: leadership is the most important tool an organisation has to make sure that people work efficiently and the organisation continues to bring more money in than is pouring out. Individual people usually look at things from quite narrow perspective, which causes their judgment to be clouded. A leader's job is to think about the bigger picture and make sure that what people do is aligned with the organisation's mission and strategy.

It is important for leaders to remember that people do not often remember the point of being at work in terms of that specific organisation's goals. People get really easily side-tracked and it is a leader's job to make sure that everyone is working towards a common goal. Clarifying the basic mission of the organisation is something that needs to be kept in mind at all times and people need to be reminded of that.

A leader also has an important role in representing the customer perspective to the employees. If customers do not need the services of an organisation, everyone in that organisation could lose their job. People often tend to look at things from the organisation's internal perspective, neglecting the customer perspective. Leaders need to make sure that everyone has what they need to fulfil those customer needs in the most productive way possible. Leaders are also needed to evaluate financial aspects of an organisation's functions. Sometimes employees want to have something that is either not needed to provide customer needs or is too expensive for the organisation to have. People tend to think about what they personally need rather than what the organisation needs in order to function properly. It is a leader's job to balance these things.

If people are put into self-guiding mode, they will quite soon forget the mission and strategy of an organisation and start to do things that please themselves. Every type of work has some nice and other not-so-nice aspects, so leaders are needed to make sure that everything runs smoothly towards the common goal. If leadership is not done properly, the operating energy of an organisation starts to slide towards internal needs.

Summary

Leadership has been a really hot topic for a long time and it doesn't seem to go away. This world has endless hunger for leaders and every single one of us can be a leader, even if we don't have a title. At a minimum, we are leaders of our own lives. Many of us are also leaders of our family. And some of us are even leaders of our workplace. Why isn't everybody behaving like a leader then? I think it is a difficult question to answer, but a lot of it comes down to our childhood, school and parents. We start as free people, but the world starts to restrain us. That happens for such a long time that we give away our right to lead our lives. That is when we start looking for leaders around us: those people who lead their lives and others' lives around them. We give them control over us. But there is a solution to that. When you start to lead without a title, you will first, claim your life back and second, become master of your own destiny. In a business context, the job of leaders is to inspire and guide others. Servant leadership is not just another fad; it is something that will bring genuine value to the workplace. What we need to be careful of is to focus on the same vision, strategy and goals. That way we can all work towards the shared outcomes.

Here are some reflective questions you can ask yourself to promote your thinking:
- How does the summary of this week's chapter contradict the ideas before? Which perspective is more valid to your opinion? Why?
- Do your leaders know what their job is?
  o Do they perform their job well?
- Do you have the right amount of leaders in your organisation?
  o Too many? Too few?
- Is your organisational hierarchy really serving you?
- Where is the customer and leaders in your organisational chart?
- Do you have self-guiding people or teams?
  o How are they performing?
- What kind of leadership would benefit them even more?
- If you just gave people the outcome to create, do you believe that people would be able to navigate to that outcome in the best possible way? Why or why not?

Write down your own thoughts here:

WEEK 22: IS BUSINESS PROCESS OUTSOURCING GOOD FOR YOUR ORGANISATION?

Business Process Outsourcing (also known as BPO) is a popular term these days, but it is not a good fit for all organisations. Most businesses are looking to reduce costs, compete with rivals and expand their customer bases by outsourcing some of their non-core business processes. It started a long time ago with the outsourcing of IT departments to other companies and today information is so easy to transfer anywhere in the world that we have seen the emergence of a wave of business process outsourcing offices all over the world.

You can find companies offering BPO for IT, HR and customer support, as well as doing routine tasks for organisations in all imaginable fields. India specialises in undertaking engineering and technical work from Western countries. China is the manufacturing plant for the whole world and the Philippines are working on administrative tasks of organisations from around the world. However, organisations have to be careful in outsourcing their business processes. You cannot just hand out important parts of your business to strangers on the other side of the world. You can use the steps listed below to evaluate if your organisation has the necessary capabilities for outsourcing some of the business processes that you need.

- Evaluate and analyse the processes that you would like to outsource. There is no point in outsourcing something that is not needed. To evaluate your processes, you can use, for example, the Customer Experience Innovation Method to figure out if those processes are really needed. Don't evaluate those processes alone, but create a team to analyse your BPO opportunities.

- Identify your core and non-core processes. Outsourcing core processes might not be a good idea, but to decide that, you need to know them.

- Analyse your organisation's capabilities for outsourcing processes. It is not just telling someone to start doing BPO; you need people, skills and technology to be successful.

- Undertake exhaustive research on which processes are real candidates for outsourcing.

- Determine what your BPO project should be like.

- Find the right company to provide BPO for you. Make sure that the contract does not limit you to put up with bad performance.

- Assign a responsible person for BPO within your organisation.

To get real benefits from BPO, you need to manage the BPO costs. There is no point in outsourcing unless you really get the same or greater value at a cheaper price. That should be based on the right KPIs and continuous follow-up. Remember to consider the potential strategic costs of BPO. If you outsource the wrong things, you might lose your organisation's capability to innovate and compete.

Selecting the right vendor for your BPO is really important. You need to determine the qualifications and features you would like to have and evaluate each potential vendor against them. Ask for proposals and make sure that you understand the contract well. In particular, keep an eye on problematic situations, how they are handled and how quickly. It might also be a good idea to have some kind of transfer period from your operators to theirs, to ensure that customers do not see the change.

Contracts are important even during good times, but they particularly come into their own when things turn problematic. According to research, up to 75% of BPO projects fail to meet the expectations of the organisation: you need a good contract. Create the contract with trust, but also give be clear regarding what responsibilities each party has. When creating the contract, consider at least: scope, SLAs, pricing, contract term, transition planning, dispute resolution, and force majeure situations.

Summary

You can outsource aspects of your business, but you cannot outsource the responsibility for your business. In some cases, you may be able to reduce the costs through BPO, but you need to be careful not to outsource the core business that brings in the money and keeps customers happy. Before making any decisions about outsourcing parts of your business processes, make a really good evaluation on what makes sense and what does not. Never outsource any of your core business processes: it is just too dangerous (unless you are going to outsource your whole business to the service provider).

Use these reflective questions to evaluate whether BPO is the right thing to do for your organisation:

- Do you have clearly identified non-core processes that could be outsourced?
- Do you have enough people, skills and technology to administer BPO?
- What are you trying to achieve with BPO?
- Who will be the responsible person in your organisation for BPO?
- Are your processes in such good shape that it is reasonable to outsource them?

- Are you outsourcing things that should not be done at all?

Write down your own thoughts here:

WEEK 23: HOW DO YOU MEANINGFULLY ALIGN YOUR REVENUE, COSTS AND SERVICE STRATEGY?

In the Business Process Management (BPM) world, the ability to simultaneously increase revenues, reduce costs and improve service is called the Triple Crown. It is a direct consequence of implementing advanced process management. And just to make the term *'process'* clear, it means everything that is done in your organisation. The twenty-first century company shifts attention from *'doing things right'* to *'doing the right things'* and, as a consequence, much of the work taking place within a company becomes *'dumb stuff'* when tested against the KPIs based on the BPM Triple Crown. This *'dumb stuff'* can be eliminated and this will typically result in cost reductions of 40–70% within three to six months of implementation across traditional processes.

A large slice of reduction is in the potential effort to run a process—the people. It also includes considerable swathes of information technology, now no longer required to manage the significantly simplified 'Outside-In' (i.e. customer-centric) processes. Savings are also available across the enterprise from reducing the need for *'outsourcing'* that does not explicitly contribute to the delivery of successful outcomes. Progressive twenty-first century companies such as Google, Apple, Gilead Sciences, Zappos, USAA and Southwest Airlines actively redeploy staff to the benefit of the bottom line—making more with less. Service improves and revenues grow.

"BPM wins the triple crown of saving money, saving time and adding value. BPM is delivering both short-term return on investment (ROI) and long-term value. One example is an insurance company that was able to reduce its claims processing costs by more than 20 percent. We are currently seeing uptake in BPM use and benefits in government, banking, health-care, transportation and travel industries," said Janelle Hill, research vice-president at Gartner (Egham, UK, March 27, 2007).

The Customer Experience Innovation Method, that is the Customer Experience Innovation Method (sometimes also called CEM, Customer Experience Method), is easy to implement and can be a very inspiring tool for meaningfully aligning your revenue, cost and service strategies quickly. It offers effective tools for analysing the successful customer outcomes (what your customers really need), moments of truth (customer interactions), breakpoints (internal handovers) and business rules (decision points). That information is put together and observed through an Outside-In lens, which reveals all the pain points in business processes and customer experience of the organisation. After that, innovation tools are used to redesign outcomes of processes to meet the customers' needs and the organisation's strategy.

The Customer Experience Innovation Method is best deployed through educating people in your organisation to understand the related concepts. The advantages of the Customer Experience Innovation Method are that it is easy to implement through facilitated workshops and it is fast to implement.

Summary

Simply put, the customer is the common denominator to everything in your business. The customer is the source of revenue as well as the source of costs. Your service strategy should be aligned to successful customer outcomes to make sure you are doing the right things. My strong suggestion is to adopt a method that will help you to map the customer journey and your internal processes, and to align everything that is done in your organisation to successful customer outcomes. You can meaningfully align revenue, costs and service strategy by leading the customer experience purposefully.

Here are some reflective questions you can ask yourself to promote your thinking:

- Do you have an efficient, fast and widely deployed method in use for managing business processes?
- Does everyone in your organisation understand the value of customer experience?
- Have you evaluated the customer interactions through a systematic method?
- Are you using metrics such as Net Promoter Score to understand what people say about your business?
- Have you mapped the processes to see what is done to create the customer outcomes?
- Have you calculated the value of life-cycle for each customer?

Write down your own thoughts here:

WEEK 24: WHAT ARE THE PROBLEMS IN LEADERSHIP?

In too many organisations, leadership is seen as something compulsory that needs to be done to please employees. Often, leaders do their "*leadership work*" on the side as an addition to doing "*the real work*". Many people also mix leadership with management. This kind of mind-set puts those leaders into half-in mode where they do only what is expected of them and even that is done poorly. It is about the time for organisations to stop accepting bad leadership and consider what would improve if those leaders were made to take the leadership role seriously. As John C. Maxwell says, "*Everything falls and rises with leadership*" and that is certainly the case in your organisation.

The picture below shows some of the common problems in leadership that I have come across. You can ask yourself how many of these are familiar in your organisation.

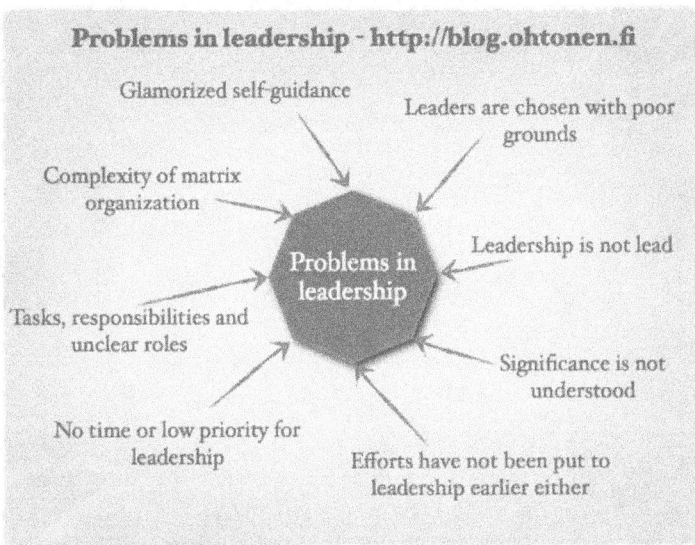

Problems in leadership - http://blog.ohtonen.fi

Glamorized self-guidance

Leaders are chosen with poor grounds

Complexity of matrix organization

Problems in leadership

Leadership is not lead

Tasks, responsibilities and unclear roles

Significance is not understood

No time or low priority for leadership

Efforts have not been put to leadership earlier either

When you are choosing your leaders, you should ask them questions about their leadership abilities and interests, not about their professional skills in whatever they are doing currently. The problems described above can be mitigated through leadership training and making great leadership really important in top management's agenda. Consider those problems you identify within the picture above; I suggest that you take five minutes for each and really think about what can you change to make the situation better.

Summary

Leadership is one of the key aspects of any organisation. If your business is a one-man-and-a-van business, you need to lead yourself. If you are an entrepreneur with a few employees, you need to lead yourself and those employees. If you are working for an international corporation, then you need to lead everyone you work with. You don't need a title for it. You don't need power or a position either. You need influence and a genuine will to be a servant leader, who helps others to grow and grows himself. It would be great if you could focus this week on your personal leadership capabilities as well as helping people around you to grow.

Here are some reflective questions you can ask yourself to promote your thinking:

- Are you really interested in leading people?
- Are you ready to function as a role model to others?
- Do you understand that leadership is a life-long learning experience?
- Is leading something you want to get better at?

Write down your own thoughts here:

WEEK 25: HOW DOES SUPPORTING A SUCCESSFUL INNER LIFE BENEFIT LEADERSHIP?

One question leaders many times ask is: how should I develop my employees? Here are some ideas on how developing employees' inner life (what goes inside them) may lead into better leadership results. People are complex beings, with different aspects to them, and this causes leaders to think about people from a more holistic perspective. Read through these ideas and think how they could affect your leadership style.

Nurture the whole person

When talking about supporting an inner life, it is not enough to support the body with exercise and the mind with training. Humans consist of what we see (body), what we think (mind or soul), and what we feel (spirit). We need to focus on all of those to get overall control of our being. Often, leadership focuses on the mind aspect of a person. That is why there are so many training events. It does not take a genius to understand why, for example, coaching is far more beneficial for personal development than training, because it focuses on the individual person, not a classroom full of different people. As a leader, you need to also focus on the body, specifically getting enough exercise (which keeps us healthy). However, we must not forget our spirit and how we feel about things either. We can affect those feels by focusing on them and analysing why we feel what we feel. Using all of these three dimensions will make us more whole.

Developing people is an iterative process, not a single project

All too often, leaders try to solve problems by sending people to a training event. That could be useful, but not always. Those mass events are generic in nature and it is impossible to organise an event which will solve everyone's situation. That is one of the reasons why coaching brings so many more substantial benefits than training. It focuses on that one individual's life. No one can be changed in one project: people develop over time. You can use, for example, group meetings, regular small group sessions, individual coaching, peer coaching, and structured solo practice to develop people. What is important is to understand that developing people takes time and is an iterative process, not a single project.

Have mindfulness included in your leadership

When talking about mindfulness, many things come into people's minds. It sounds, once again, like one of those hype-driven fads that come and go.

However, you do not have to call what you do by any specific name. It is more important what you try to achieve. You need to focus on the reflection on and selection of a specific capacity or quality you want to work on (for example, courage or patience). Then you can practise self-observation on those capacities that you want to develop. After that, it is hard work to turn insight into deliberate, dedicated, daily practice. Some people say that well-planned is half done, but that is not true. If you have a plan in your drawer, it will not do any good: you need to transform the plan into action and make it part of your daily activity.

Everyone deserves to grow

Do not leave anyone behind in your organisation. Get everyone involved and encourage those actions to be voluntary. Those people who participate in the programme need to be willing to improve their lives and to think about their inner life from more a holistic perspective. And I bet that when people start to fix their inner lives, they will be happier and that will lead to better leadership results.

Do not try to grow alone

Some people might be good at doing things alone, but they will be great when working together. People do not grow as effectively via on-line training, reading a book or just taking in information. There is an exponential impact in having people grow and learn together. When people do things alone, they tend to get stuck with their own ideas. But when there are more people around, the discussion and learning experience grows with different thought patterns.

Summary

It is more important what kind of person you are from within rather than what you look like from the outside (in some situations, that is important too). It is really beneficial for the business to help people grow as individuals through improving their inner lives. Even though this week's chapter has several good tips to help you to do that, there is no one right way to make it happen. You need to start to look for ways to contribute to others. I strongly suggest building a growing mentality in your organisation. The results will not come overnight, so thinking of it as a process instead of a project helps to keep the focus and you will reap the benefits in the long term. Remember that every single person you have near you deserves to grow. It is your responsibility to help people around you to become better versions of themselves. That way you will both benefit from the growth.

Here are some reflective questions you can ask yourself to promote your thinking:

- What could you change to start supporting the inner life of your employees?
- Do you build character within yourself?
- Do you help others to build their character?
- Have you evaluated what is going on inside you?
- How do you take care of your body, mind and soul? Or are you lacking in some of those areas?
- Does your organisation use training to grow skills of people or to solve problems?
- Have you identified your strengths? If the answer is yes, do you work through them?
- Have you identified your weaknesses? If the answer is yes, what are you doing to develop them?
- How would regular self-evaluation and observation help you to improve yourself?
- Do you innovate in teams? Or is it left up to individuals? How would changing the way you innovate benefit you?

Write down your own thoughts here:

WEEK 26: HOW CAN DEFERENCE BE A GOOD LEADERSHIP STYLE?

Have you ever heard, or even said, that you do not get enough appreciation in your organisation? Many people might even prefer an appropriate and well timed "thank you" from their manager rather than a small salary increase. People are eager to be valued for what they do. Here are some ideas that you can use to think about whether deference will work for you as a leadership style.

Notice what others are doing right and thank them for that

Do not walk around the office with your eyes closed. Talk to people; find out what they are good at and where they succeed. Then praise them for that! If you do not know where to start, you can look at the numbers and praise based on them. You can also think about the positive qualities of each person and praise for positive behaviour (reward for what you want to see more of). Consider each employee and evaluate what he or she brings personally into organisation. Mark these things into your mind and thank them for that. If you come up with a situation where you need to give some constructive feedback, do it alone.

Here is a personal story of mine related to leadership: I used to praise everyone for everything good they did. People really liked that. But my mistake was that I also gave negative feedback (not always in a constructive form) so that everyone heard it. Over time, that led to a situation where people could not be sure what they might get from me in public situations. That also damaged the good feedback I was giving. One day, this backfired on me badly and I was forced to change my ways. I decided that I would give good feedback publicly and constructive (no more negative at all) feedback face-to-face (no e-mails, calls, etc.). That has been a very successful strategy. Now people do not get negative feedback publicly and having a face-to-face discussion does not mean something bad.

Think about the physician's oath: "Above all else, do no harm"

Unfortunately, as people we are so imperfect that we will always do some harm. Therefore, what I suggest is to do as little harm as possible. Even in hard situations where you need to get something difficult done with others, think first and then act. Try to evaluate the long-term implications of your actions. Furthermore, make sure that you do not devalue anyone, even by accident. Sometimes employees can be real pain, but you need to be a professional leader and try to find a way to change the situation so that it serves you both without mental violence.

Be an appreciative leader

Think about the ways that you show your appreciation to your employees. Do you give out public rewards? Do you send handwritten thank you notes? Do you give a pat on the back for a job well done? Do you give out dinner cards? Or something else? The more specific you can be about what you value in your employees, and the more you notice what is most meaningful to that employee, the more positive your impact on that person is likely to be. Get personal in your appreciation.

Start appreciation with yourself

You cannot value others if you do not value yourself. At the end of the day, stop for a moment to ask yourself "*What can I rightly feel proud of today?*" and "*What could I do better tomorrow?*". Be appreciative for yourself in the same manner as you are for others. One caveat is that you should avoid being a leader that expects respect back. If you give something, give it with a sincere heart and do not expect favours in return.

Summary

Studies have found that up to 70% of people leave a company citing lack of deference as a reason. I find it incredible how we as leaders are not able to show our appreciation to other people well enough. We just forget the good old "*please*" and "*thank you*" too easily. To fix that, I believe most of us need to be more attached to the current moment and be grateful to the people around us. When someone does something good, let's praise them! And if they don't perform that well, let's help them.

Here are some reflective questions you can ask yourself to promote your thinking:

- What would this kind of leadership style do for you?
- Would you like to take a week and try it out to see what kind of results you will get?

Write down your own thoughts here:

WEEK 27: HOW CAN YOU THINK YOUR WAY TO SUCCESS?

Success is something that comes from within you. This week's chapter presents some thinking patterns that you can change to make your life more successful. Nothing good comes without work, so each one of these steps is a big one and will require you to work hard. But I believe that the reward is worth it, since every step along the way will take you closer to success.

Do not think, do or say bad things

You get back what you put in. If you have bad manners, you think badly of others, you speak badly of others or do bad things, then that is what you are going to get. Test yourself: try to go one day without thinking, doing or saying bad things. How hard do you find it? I can say that for me it takes quite a lot of effort to go an entire day without doing or even thinking one bad thought. When you think good thoughts, do good things and say good things, then you will see the benefits. Other people will like you more and are more likely to work with you. In short, adopt a more positive mind-set.

Value what you already have

Do now always pine after what you do not have. Value what you have and use it in the best way you can. One dime in a wise man's hand is worth much more than a dime in an ignorant man's hand. Even little things can bring you great rewards when used correctly. When you train your brain to be more thankful for what you have, you will become happier and more positive. That will bring more good things in your life.

Hold your integrity in every situation

Do you have several "faces"? Have one face and wear it proudly with integrity. When you know who you are and why you think the way you do, then you can face any situation without a problem or internal conflicts. But if you have one face at work and another one at home, you will have to change between these profiles and that will consume energy. Create your own identity and integrity so that you are able to follow it even under stress. Change your thinking so that you evaluate situations based on your own internal values.

Have big plans for your future

Do not settle for mediocrity. Have big plans for your future and succeed in getting them through well-planned roadmaps. Your dreams will become goals when you make a plan for how to get there. If you strive for little things, that is what you will get. If you strive for big things, that is what you will get. Change your thinking so that you are thinking about the big picture rather than the small steps.

Keep your plans up-to-date

Regularly update your roadmap. Mount it on your walls, change it when needed, prioritise things based on your goals and never lose sight of the target. Be persistent and work hard. People are good at starting things, but finishing is the goal that will give the reward, so do not get lost on the way. Prioritise everything you do based on your big plans and do not let other people take control of your life. That requires changing your thinking so that you are present in the moment and able to evaluate what is going on at all times.

Summary

We are what we think. We get what we think. We attract people who are aligned to what we think. Is that enough of a pep talk for you to start thinking about what you think? For me it was. It is extremely hard (at least for me), but it is also extremely useful to think only positive and constructive thoughts. There is no use in dwelling on the past or negative thoughts. I cannot stress that enough. The first step is to start being grateful. Each day, write down something that you are grateful for. I am sure you can find something. Eventually, you will find more and more things to be grateful for. It will help you to focus on the positive things in your life. If you have problems, solve them, don't dwell on them. I wish you happy thoughts!

Here are some reflective questions you can ask yourself to promote your thinking:
- How do these ideas work for you?
- Do you have already something you think you should start working on to be more successful?
- Test yourself: try to have one day during which you do not think, do or say bad things.
- What are you grateful for today?

Write down your own thoughts here:

WEEK 28: HOW CAN RULES CONTRIBUTE TO ORGANISATIONAL INTEGRITY?

Many businesses seem to struggle to achieve an appropriate balance between maintaining rules and discipline while providing employees with enough space and freedom to pursue their individual wishes. Some organisations are far too permissive, allowing their personnel to do virtually anything as they see fit. Others are too strict, severely restricting their staff's actions and behaviour. Remote offices and home-working has not made this situation easier.

Here is a formula to consider: Rules + Relationships = Organisational Integrity

My years of experience in the business world have taught me that this balance is crucial for a healthy, productive working environment. If you have rules, but have very little in terms of relationships, it is likely that you will experience rebellion.

If, on the other hand, you have placed a strong emphasis on relationships, but you do not have considered, established guidelines for daily practices and behaviour, you could experience chaos. Being able to balance the two provides assurance to your people that you care about them, yet at the same time expect them to produce results in keeping with your company's mission and values.

Problems occur in your organisation when there is confusion among employees as to what *"to do things right"* means. As leaders, it is our responsibility to communicate that clearly and effectively. Business and professional people look to their leaders to define the parameters under which they are expected to perform their jobs well.

Rules and guidelines, especially when created with valued input from the people who will be governed by them, are not restrictive. They are actually empowering because the individuals understand they are free to use their talents and abilities within those limits. Without those rules, employees can become confused by the fear of doing something wrong.

Establishing rules just for the sake of controlling people can be demoralising, so guidelines must be used as a means of enhancing the productivity—and satisfaction—of your employees. Strong, effective leaders know how to balance compassion and discipline. Are you such a leader?

Summary

Both rules and relationships in an organisation are important. You need to find an optimal balance between them. The rules should help people to succeed in their job rather than suppress them. Rules should bring stability and reliability instead of restrictions and bureaucracy. Relationships between people in your organisation are important. People need to get the work done together and in a constructive way. This means they need to be able to trust each other. Appropriate rules will serve to enable that, but unsuitable rules may make it more difficult to work together. I suggest periodic evaluation of all the known business rules in the organisation to make sure that the rules are still valid and make sense.

Here are some reflective questions you can ask yourself to promote your thinking:

- What gets the strongest emphasis where you work: rules or relationships? Explain how you see this being demonstrated on a day-to-day basis.
- How do you think a leader can go about seeking this balance between rules and relationships? Is it even practical to attempt this, in your opinion? Why or why not?
- Have you ever found yourself in a situation where you were not certain what the rules were that governed your actions or the plans you were formulating? If so, how did you feel about that circumstance—and what was the outcome?

Write down your own thoughts here:

WEEK 29: HOW CAN BUSINESS COACHING HELP YOUR ORGANISATION TO SUCCEED?

Soon enough you will be planning how your organisation's Euro, Pounds or whatever are going to be spent to educate your employees and expand your personal knowledge base so that you are on the cutting edge. Maybe you are using a traditional way to spend it… on cattle call seminars at some cold, uninviting hotel, where the speakers drone on and on and on. Alternatively, you could spend it on tailor-made, personalised business coaching with proven results. Let me take a few minutes to make the case for business coaching as an example of the most effective way to spend your limited resources.

First, let's talk about the familiar, traditional seminars:
- It basically involves traditional lectures: Boring! Ordinarily, the biggest benefit from traditional training is to get away from the office's buzz and to get time to think.
- One-size-fits-all speeches: maybe they fit your organisation's needs, maybe they don't. But they rarely meet your personal needs.
- The information presented tends to be general rather than specific because the audience is made up of different organisations.
- It's not financially the best option. Research has shown that traditional training is not very effective.
- Feel free to add your own negative points like "it's tedious," "it's not interactive", "the food is terrible", etc.

Now, let's talk about business coaching and why it is a better fit for your company:
- Business coaching is tailored to your specific needs. This process can be designed just for your inner circle or for your entire organisation. You decide what you want based on your needs and objectives.
- Business coaching is interactive. You go through a series of 'hands-on' exercises and activities, which help you assess where you are and where you want to go. This is a fun and exciting event or series of events, NOT a lecture.
- The information presented by a seasoned business coach is specific to your company and your industry niche, NOT generalised.
- You decide on the venue, the participants, the timetable and the format for business coaching. It is not a pre-set agenda that is forced down your throat or scheduled at the 'most inconvenient time.' One key to participating in business coaching is to design the process so

that it's at the best time, when your key players are available to be active participants.

- It's financially the option because you will be able to move your organisation forward quickly and see benefits immediately. The process is personalised to sync with your company's vision, and to enhance your company goals and objectives.

- According to research, coaching is a far more effective method of raising productivity than traditional training.

Let me give you an example. Let's say that you have formed a team to work on a new project. This team has never worked together before. It brings together an employee from IT, finance, HR, design, and logistics. These employees are exceptional individuals. There is just one problem, they are each leaders in their respective departments and when they are thrown together, you have concerns that everyone is going to try to jockey into position to be 'the leader' and they won't be collaborative and work well as a team.

This scenario cannot be handled in a leadership seminar. You need a trained business coach to get in the trenches with your people to assess their strengths and weaknesses as individuals, so that they can be plugged in for maximum effectiveness in the team. The business coach also assists them in clarifying the vision for the project, and in setting goals and action steps for carrying the project through to success.

Summary

A personalised business coach can really help you to tap into the hidden resources within you, not to mention the passion that you can awaken. Training is good in some cases, but if you really want to know yourself better and discover your own limits, then coaching can help you to find and push those. I have used business coaches for several years and I think it has been the best money I have spent. I have seen growth on a personal level as well as in my business life. I have been even able to change my own behaviour to support my goals better. Some say "the sky is the limit", but I think they should say "you are your own limit". Get a business coach who will help you to become a better you. You deserve it!

Here are some reflective questions you can ask yourself to promote your thinking:

- What are the biggest obstacles on your way to success?
- Are you doing your 'dream' work? What is stopping you from doing it?

Write down your own thoughts here:

WEEK 30: WHAT ARE THE IMPORTANT QUESTIONS IN BUSINESS PROCESS MANAGEMENT PROJECTS?

Starting a Business Process Management (BPM) project and choosing the right BPM System (BPMS) can be quite tricky. There are several methods available to choose from. This week's entry presents some questions that you can ask when thinking about starting a BPM project.

What process is at hand and what does it achieve?

You should first get an idea what that process is about. Asking what it achieves will help you identify the reason why this process exists. It will also help you to understand how critical this process is for the organisation's customers. The process should clearly contribute to producing successful customer outcomes (SCO).

How does the process currently work?

To choose what is going on in the process, you should get some kind of idea of how that process works today. There are many ways to do that: for example, a flowchart, or even better using the Customer Experience Innovation (CEI) Method. If your organisation does not have process maps, this is a good time to pick up a pen and start drawing. But remember that the point is not to get that process map, but to understand how that process works today. Therefore, it is important to have all relevant parties participating in the process mapping. You can ask Outside-In consultants to assist you with workshops.

Who are the participants in the process and what are their roles?

This will get you the roles and responsibilities of the people involved in the process. This will also help you to find the right performers for various tasks. The right people should be doing the right work.

Which business units participate in the process?

This will help you to understand who the stakeholders will be and how complex it will be to design the process. The general rule is that if there are more business units (silos), the process will be more complex and the more effort you (and client project team) will spend bringing everyone to a common accepted stage. The more you have silos in your organisation, the more complicated it will be. A part of Outside-In thinking is to get rid of those useless silos and design the organisation's hierarchy around the successful customer outcomes.

What will the value of the process be to customers in the future?

Now you can start asking questions about what needs to be built. Consider what business you are in, what the successful customer outcome is and how to provide that with minimal moments of truth. In this part you will get the full benefits of the Customer Experience Innovation Method.

Where does the process start and end?

This is very important, maybe even the most important question once you have established what business are you in. Sometimes you will realise that employees do not understand where the process starts and where it ends for your customers. They just know their part of the process.

What information flows from one person to another?

This will help you to model and minimise internal handovers (so-called breakpoints). If you are going to use a BPMS, this will help you determine what the screen and data fields should be. You could be dealing with complex sets of data. Ask questions about why these information flows happen and whether they are really useful.

Which internal and external systems will this process interact with?

Find out what level of integrations you are looking for. Most of the business process will be integrated with other systems. Sometimes integrations could lead to complex processes, screens and routing. Remember that integration is a tool for facilitating the provision of successful customer outcomes.

Are there any business rules associated with the process?

Ask what business rules there are. Also ask how often they change. And most importantly, ask whether they are still relevant. If you are going to use a rule engine as part of the BPMS, this will help you determine if rules should be embedded into the process or put in as a separate component.

What are your reporting requirements?

Your data layouts and your process routing could depend upon what reporting requirements there are. If a user needs business reports unit-wise or region-wise, you will need to incorporate those fields into your workflow.

When you measure, remember that you get what you measure. It is crucial that your KPIs are aligned with successful customer outcomes.

What are your implementation time lines and constraints?

Determine the time lines and constraints. It is possible that people will ask you the question *"when can I have this?"*. Be sure that you keep it open-ended or at least realistic. Unless your implementation team has analysed everything, do not give an estimate. Determine what constraints the organisation has and figure out how the project can still go through.

Who will sign off on the requirements, user acceptance testing and final production for this process?

Finding the right people is important. If one person is going to sign off on the requirements and the other is going to do user acceptance testing then you are in trouble. Make sure the right stakeholders are in your list and you spend enough time talking to them over the course of project implementation. It is very important to make sure that top management is committed to process improvement and their full support is behind the project.

Summary

BPM projects, like everything else in your life, should start with the end in mind. The goals of the processes and business should be very clear before starting to do anything about them. Otherwise, you may end up doing the wrong things. You need to evaluate the goals and current situation to understand the BPM problem area better. Then you can formulate solutions and a roadmap to improve them. Remember to include all the relevant stakeholders in the project and make sure they are committed at the level required. Communication is a very important part of BPM projects, so remember to make a communication plan that clearly indicates what will be communicated to which stakeholders.

Here are some reflective questions you can ask yourself to promote your thinking:
- What is your current situation in terms of process efficiency and effectiveness?
- How do your processes help to create great customer experiences?
- Are employees happy with the current state of processes or would they like to improve something?

- How are business rules aligned to processes, and processes to customer strategy?
- Do you have a lot of waste (useless work) in your processes? How could you remove them?

Write down your own thoughts here:

WEEK 31: WOULD YOU RATHER HAVE LONG-TERM VALUE THAN SHORT-TERM FROM YOUR BUSINESS?

Many business owners seem to have so-called "*give it to me now*" syndrome, focusing too much on getting as much as possible for themselves from their business. Contemporary shareholders demand that executives maximise shareholder value as much as possible. That shareholder value is typically measured by share price: meaning the share price today, not the share price next quartile or next year. This very narrow perspective on raising stock price by any means possible keeps companies from making long-term investments, protecting the interests of essential stakeholders like employees and customers, or taking much account of social welfare and ethical considerations in the making of business decisions.

Those managers who understand the flaw in this short-term perspective can act against it. This week's chapter presents some practical ways to do that. One is to educate shareholders by providing them with better information about their own long-term interests. Another one can be to practise so-called shareholder selection. The third is to ensure that managers are not rewarded in such a way that makes them think too much about the short-term demands of the shareholders.

Educating shareholders

Most shareholders are saving for the long term, to retire, or to pay a child's tuition fees and they are people who care about the quality of the air they breathe and the ecological health of the planet they leave for future generations. Most of these long-term, diverse, socially concerned shareholders do not want their companies to maximise short-term share prices when it means greater harm to long-term growth, the value of their other investments, or society and the environment. The problem in this equation is that the only information these investors see is the share price, so that is the only thing they can focus on. If executives want shareholders to understand their own interests, corporations need to educate their shareholders by providing more and better quality information about the company's need to invest in its future, the importance of maintaining good relationships with stakeholders, and the company's commitment to ethical and socially responsible behaviour. Organisations should talk more about how they add value to others like their customers and employees.

Shareholder selection

At least one powerful type of shareholder is one who is not diversified, does not seem to care about ethics or social responsibility, and prefers to hold shares for a maximum of two or three years. This powerful minority are activist hedge funds. With all due respect to hedge fund managers, the nature of their job is to take strong positions in a few companies, do everything possible to raise the share price, then get out. This means that hedge fund interests clash with those of long-term, diversified, prosocial (investing in others) investors. If the latter are the kind of investors you want, you need to discourage short-term investors from buying shares in the first place.

Rewards for adding long-term value

If you want your organisation's managers, directors and executives to focus on the future and behave in a socially responsible fashion, it is essential to make sure that reward plans do not rely too heavily on share price as a performance metric. There is no need for short-term shareholders to pressure managers to raise the share price when that is not what determines managerial compensation. You get what you reward for, and if your executive "*pay for performance*" compensation scheme rewards managers for short-term and socially irresponsible behaviour, it should come as no surprise when that's what you get. Organisations should focus more on compensation that is based on successful customer outcomes that the organisation provides.

Summary

Long-term focus on value can help organisations to retain their employees and customers easier. It also enables the organisation to evaluate their social and environmental effects better. Leaders need to start thinking more about the long-term value they can build rather than the short-term quartile profits. It is better to have £1m tomorrow than £1,000 today. Educating stakeholders to see the long-term value the organisation could create can alleviate the pressure created by them to generate short-term value. Furthermore, favouring such stakeholders who do not mind being in for the long-term benefits will help to facilitate the generation of lasting business. Employees, leaders and other internal staff should be rewarded for creating lasting value instead of quick-fix solutions. Maximising the value of a customer through their whole life cycle is more profitable than short-term bad financial transaction.

Here are some reflective questions you can ask yourself to promote your thinking:
- How could your organisation focus more on long-term value?
- What does long-term value mean in your organisation?

Write down your own thoughts here:

WEEK 32: DOES MORE INTERACTION MEAN IMPROVED CUSTOMER EXPERIENCE?

Discussion about good and bad customer service experiences (particularly bad ones) is a favourite topic of many coffee table conversations. In the world of Outside-In (customer-centric), we call these customer interactions 'moments of truth'. Based on Outside-In thinking, the management of those moments of truth are one of the key factors to success and listed below are some reasons for that.

- *Customer interaction.* Every time a customer interacts with your organisation, it is an opportunity for them to form an impression, which may be either a good or bad one.
- *Surplus costs.* Every moment of truth is a cost to the organisation, because you have to work to produce that moment of truth.
- *For every customer interaction there is at least one moment of truth.* If customers have too many bad 'moments of truth', or 'moments of misery' as they may be called, the likely result is that the customer will leave, or at least seriously think about leaving, your business.
- *Less is more.* The more moments of truth it takes to get something done within your organisation, the less successful the customer experience and the more likely it is that the customer will leave. The more you have those customer interactions, the higher the probability of producing moments of misery.
- *Optimising your process.* For every customer experience that deserves to exist (i.e. they create value for the customer and profit for the company), there are an optimum number of moments of truth (i.e. customer interactions). The customer experience is the process that you need to manage.

I recently had an episode with an administrator of our flat. For some reason there was no heat in the radiator of our bathroom. And it is not nice to have showers in a freezing cold bathroom, so I rang up to the administrator. He said that he was too busy to take care of it and he would get back to me 'asap'. Well, I left Finland for a one-week trip. I returned home to find that the radiator still didn't work. I sent an e-mail and called the administrator. He did not respond. I sent more e-mails.

After another week, a repairman came to fix that radiator. It took him about seven minutes to fix the problem. However, before that it took me several e-mails and calls, several cold showers, and a lot of hassle to get that repairman to come. Furthermore, I pay decent money every month for that service.

From my perspective, this could have been just one interaction. Going back to the list, there was a point about how the more moments of truth it takes to get something done, the less successful the customer experience will be. Certainly having to call and e-mail several times and still not having the problem resolved made me feel like the experience was less than successful.

The list touches on the point that every moment of truth is a cost to the organisation. Every time I called the administrator, I encountered a number of moments of truth. The costs to the organisation are not always obvious, but in this example they include making telecommunication available, having someone to answer available, providing an e-mail system to send out follow-up e-mails and contact the repairman, just to name some obvious ones that I encountered during my interactions.

When challenging most customer experience management professionals about how they would improve the customer experience for this interaction, they talk about making each touchpoint better, ensuring the business support people are as helpful as possible and capturing the survey results, feeding them back into the customer experience management programme and employee rewards programme.

Ask most consultancies how they could improve this customer experience and in most cases, their approaches will be the same. They would assume this customer process deserves to exist because it is not possible to stop customers. Thus, using traditional approaches, they would create a project to design an improved experience for customers. Then they would ensure that each customer's interaction is 'better' and 'quicker' and will reward customer service agents for their increased 'efficiency', their KPIs being aligned to the average touch time and talk time, or the speed they can get customers off the phone.

Here is the catch. This whole customer interaction could have been made significantly better and significantly cheaper by considering the philosophy of whether this customer experience deserved to exist. Instead of having the administrator as a middleman, a significantly better customer experience would have been to enable me to call the repairman directly when I experienced problems. This approach could have helped to solve the problem quicker and in most cases, could have prevented the need for customers to call the administrator. In addition, this approach simultaneously reduces the cost of maintaining support systems and personnel and significantly improves the customer experience, since I would have got my radiator fixed much quicker.

This kind of Outside-In customer-focused thinking is being used by many of this century's most successful companies and the Customer Experience Innovation (CEI) Method is one technique which is enabling organisations to benefit from this approach. So when asked to improve the customer experience, never assume that all customer experiences deserve to exist: you have to challenge them.

Summary

It is far better to focus on the quality of customer interactions instead of the quantity. Your organisation exists to serve its customers; therefore, every interaction with the customers should be made useful, meaningful, easy and fun. It is better to keep the interactions to a minimum to ensure that you will not deteriorate the relationship. Every interaction is a potential moment of magic or misery. Make sure they are moments of magic (delighting the customer).

Here are some reflective questions you can ask yourself to promote your thinking:

- Have you mapped out the journey your customers take?
- Have you purposefully evaluated all the customer interactions your organisation creates?
- Have you evaluated which customer interactions are moments of magic and which ones are moments of misery?
- Has your organisation optimised the number of customer interactions it requires to render the service or products?
- Have you calculated how much customer interactions cost your organisation?

Write down your own thoughts here:

WEEK 33: CAN YOUR ORGANISATION PRODUCE ENDLESS CREATIVITY?

Selling creativity to organisations is quite easy, because there is unlimited demand for it. Who wouldn't want to improve their business at any given moment? But there are no authorities watching over this creativity creation and even companies who sell creativity seem to get stuck every now and then. But isn't it so that when the organisation is having its roughest time, people start to innovate new things, because they have to? That is not true of creativity however, since it is done under pressure. Organisations that show true creativity dismantle and rebuild their processes from time to time to make better structures. It doesn't mean that those organisations should run around like headless chickens renewing their processes just for the sake of doing it.

But renewing organisations processes is most definitely needed and it must be nicer to do it when things are still alright rather than when it is too late. What should the perspective on innovating the processes be then? Effectiveness, productivity, etc? If we think about the question about why those processes exist, maybe we will find the answer. The customer is the reason for any business organisation to exist. And those working in the public sector might think that it doesn't involve them, but they are wrong. Even in the public sector, money comes from somewhere and is used to do something with. Therefore, there must a customer too!

When we start to innovate processes based on the customers and what they really need, we get into the very source of business. People interact with your organisation because you fulfil some need for them. And those who do it best will get the most clients. How can organisations have endless creativity then? Certainly, knowing their customers really well and being able to think outside of the box how to fill their needs. There is a Customer Experience Innovation (CEI) method available that will let you do this in a controlled manner.

Summary

Organisations can have endless creativity, but it comes at a price. It takes effort and time, not to mention skills, to keep people in creative mode. The best thing to do is to build the creativity into the organisational culture, so that it becomes part of daily life.

Here are some reflective questions you can ask yourself to promote your thinking:

- How could your organisation become more creative?
- Is innovation a domain for the gifted few or for everyone?
- How are feedback and suggestions handled?
- Who is responsible for developing your organisation? Who should it be and why?
- How could you become more creative personally?

Write down your own thoughts here:

WEEK 34: HOW CAN CHANGE MANAGEMENT ENSURE SUCCESS IN BPM?

Based on extensive literature research in scientific journals, I have found the following factors related to change management perspective to be relevant for an organisation to succeed in Business Process Management (BPM) endeavours. You can read through this list and think about how these matters are relevant to your organisation.

The reward system adjusts to serve the employees after the changes

People do what they get rewarded for. When you undertake process improvement in your organisation, remember to keep your reward system up-to-date and reward people only for the results that you want to achieve in your organisation. Actually, when you want to change something, you should change the reward system first so that people are eager to change things rather than staying with the old ways.

There are training and/or educational programmes to update employees' skills

People need to have good skills relevant to their jobs. When you train employees, it does not just increase happiness; it will also help you to get your change programmes through easier. That is because people do what they know and if you do not train them to know new things, the status quo will reign.

BPM concepts and methodologies are known and understood

BPM is not a very clearly defined term. It will mean different things in different organisations. Therefore, you should train your people to know the basic concepts and methods, so there will be common language to talk about change programmes. This also includes top management, which should have and use the same language as employees do.

The project plan for reengineering processes is adequate

You should start with the end in mind. How do you change your organisation from the current situation to the new one? Do you have enough resources? Is there enough time, money and so on, to make the change programme successfully?

People are eager to improve the existing state of processes

The culture of the organisation should be 'change positive'. When people are rewarded for change and they are taught to embrace positive change, then change programmes will be easier and faster. People will resist what they are afraid of, so feed the atmosphere of questioning current state of processes and foster the ideas that people have for improvements.

Summary

There is no change resistance, there are only unappealing options. You need to build change as part of the organisation, because it is the only inevitable thing that will persist. Reward people for fostering change and improving how things are done. Teach them how to become better change agents for the whole organisation. Big things start from something small, so do not neglect them. Use BPM tools to keep the processes efficient and encourage people to improve the existing state of processes and things that are done.

You can reflect on the above-mentioned factors against your organisation with the following thought-provoking questions:
- What are your people rewards based upon?
- Do you ask employees for new ideas and implement them?
- Do you have training programmes for BPM?
- Is your customer experience aligned with process improvements?
- Are your employees eager to improve the processes that you have now?

Write down your own thoughts here:

WEEK 35: HOW CAN YOU BUILD YOUR CHARACTER AS A LEADER?

It is very important to develop your character as a leader, and there are some factors that are related to this. You may want to take a few minutes and think about the following factors and how you could apply them in your life to become better leader.

Recognise your own strengths and then develop and work through your strengths

We are all good at something and if you start using your strengths as your leverage, you will become a better leader. Lead people through your strengths. Have you ever really thought what your strengths are and how exactly you use them?

Courage to lead

A good leader does not necessarily always know what they should do or have all the answers, but they have courage to lead people, take the initiative, start things and learn along the way. As a leader, you do not always have to be right or know everything, but you need to have enough courage to take controlled risks and help people to do their best.

Decisive guidance: controlling uncertainty

We live in very volatile times and that creates a need for good leadership. Having a clear goal and guiding decisively towards that goal helps people to control uncertainty.

Coaching and mentoring

We can be great, even one of the best, but we can never be as good alone as we can with other people and with help. Recognise your needs, where you could develop yourself, and get yourself a mentor and coach. They are not the same thing, so have someone experienced as your mentor and someone trained as your coach. If you would like to get your own coach, you can contact us, since we have certified coaches who will gladly help you to succeed.

Investing into you

To build your character as a leader, you need to invest in yourself before you can invest in others. What you do should be something you can be proud of years later and to do that in every situation you need to develop yourself all the time. In the end, the only thing that matters is who you are.

Summary

Our character reveals who we really are. It sets the foundations of how we think, what we say and what we do. Building your character regardless of your position is very important to succeed in life. We have both good and bad character traits and when things get tough, we need those good character traits to get over the hurdles. Have the courage and passion to become a better character each day. Analyse what your character traits are and then build on the good ones and diminish the bad ones. It might help to get a coach; it will open your eyes to a different side to things and therefore expand your world.

Ask yourself some of these questions and think about the consequences of your answers in relation to your life:

- Have I already found my strengths? Am I working through them?
- How has my character developed in the past?
- How will I invest in myself?
- Do I add value to others?

Write down your own thoughts here:

WEEK 36: DOES BETTER COMMUNICATION CONTRIBUTE TO SUCCESS IN BPM?

I'm sure you have heard the phrase 'communicate, communicate, communicate' many times. But still quite many studies show that managers do not communicate enough to their staff, companies do not communicate enough to their clients and so on. This is also the case in Business Process Management. Below are most important views related to communication in Business Process management. These were identified through scientific research that I did for my doctorate thesis.

There is open communication between supervisors and their subordinates

Nowadays, open communication is key to success in BPM. Employees will know what is going on in a practical level anyway, so there is no need for managers to hide things from them. An organisation has to be built on trust and if you have some reason not to trust your people, you need to do something about that in order to get open communication.

Co-workers have confidence and trust in each other

It is not enough that supervisors and subordinates trust each other; co-workers, that is people on the same level, also need to be able to trust each other. They have to be sure that everybody does their part of the job and no one is left behind. That will help them to innovate and foster the change continuously.

Teamwork between co-workers is the typical way to solve problems

There should not be a single point of problem solving, but everyone should work together to find solutions to problems. No single person can come up with solutions as elegant as a team can, because everyone knows different things and have different ideas.

There is performance recognition among co-workers

People should pat each other on the back when they do something well. A reward system within in an organisation is one thing and performance recognition among co-workers is another. People should give feedback to each other—negative feedback privately and positive feedback publicly. Making mistakes should be allowed and successes should be praised.

Customer expectations are considered in discussions about the organisation

The customer is the key factor for everyone, and that really means everyone, in the organisation. And the customer should not be implicitly thought to be inside the project; the whole project should be created for the customer explicitly. Everyone should know what the customers expect from them.

Summary

Both in business process and leadership initiatives, communication is really important. It is probably the most important factor, because communication shapes the way people discuss and think about things. Having open communication between management and employees helps to alleviate problems and to celebrate victories. It is no secret that teamwork can be a more effective way of operating processes than individuality. People can also innovate and solve problems quicker in a team. To promote open communication in your teams, encourage people to appraise one another. You should also have continuous conversations about the different aspects related to customers with your staff (how they see things).

You can use the following example questions to come up with some ideas on improving your organisation with better communication and collaboration:

- Do you have open communication culture?
- Do you trust your colleagues? Do they trust you?
- Do you have confidence in the people in your organisation?
- Do they all have confidence in each other?
- Do you praise other people's good work?
- Do you solve problems together?
- Does everyone in your organisation know what customers expect from him or her?
- Does everyone live up to the customer expectations of their work?

Write down your own thoughts here:

WEEK 37: IS YOUR BUSINESS TRUSTWORTHY IN THE EYES OF THE CUSTOMER?

How are the trust levels that your customers or clients have in your company as the economic uncertainty continues around the world?

Some time ago, a company called Edelman, did some significant research about a variety of issues related to the global marketplace, concluded an extensive study asking a cross-section of people to express their present levels of confidence in corporate executives and their companies. In similar surveys in the past, respondents had pointed to "*financial performance*" and "*quality products*" as some of the most important attributes that influence their trust in those organisations. Since the worldwide economic collapse, however, the significance of those factors has fallen dramatically. The key issues now include "*transparent and honest practices*" and "*being a company I can trust*".

It appears that many people now realise just because a business can demonstrate outstanding financial performance, this does not necessarily reflect on its dependability. In other words, if you cannot trust the people producing impressive economic numbers, what difference does it make?

In recent years, the credibility of many sectors of the business and professional world has taken a major hit. "*Who can we trust?*" is a question many of us have asked, and sadly that question has not always been easy to answer. From the top leaders in government to celebrated corporate executives to rising entrepreneurs, integrity and honesty seem to have become qualities found in diminishing supply.

You may remember that 80% of CEOs think that they produce a great customer experience and only about 8% of their customers agreed. As you can see, there is a huge gap between the perceived and provided service. That kind of gap makes your business less trustworthy in the eyes of your customers. Have you done surveys measuring the gap between your own expectations and customers'? Do you know what your customers actually expect from you?

Summary

What can we learn from this? One might suggest that if you desire to build and sustain a strong organisational reputation, you and your team should make your actions trustworthy, diligent and impeccably honest. That would be the base for earning your customers' trust. After that you should start measuring and evaluating the customer experience that your customers expect to have and what you are actually providing.

Here are some reflective questions you can ask yourself to promote your thinking:

- Do your customers trust your business?
- Do you generate more bad (at the customer's expense) or good (willingly and fully paid) profits?
- How ethical is your business?
- Does your company care about "green values" and taking care of nature?
- Are employees proud to work in your organisation?
- Are you being realistic about your customers' expectations?

Write down your own thoughts here:

WEEK 38: HAVE YOU THOUGHT ABOUT SECRETS TO PERSONAL SUCCESS?

How would you define success for yourself? Have you spent some time thinking about what it really means to you?

There are many ways to define success: status, power, promotions and money, among others. But one important measure of success is impact—i.e. the influence individuals have on the people surrounding them, whether in the workplace, the community, or their own homes. What difference has their life had on others? And what are they doing to add value to others?

Even though many of us devote our lives to pursuits in the materialistic or business and professional world, there are other possibilities. The following are some success factors that may change the direction of your life if you want to.

Sense of direction

To achieve success, it is important to know where you are going: what your goals and objectives are. Make a personal mission statement and identify the roles in your life. What do you really want to achieve in your life?

Understanding

We need to be able to deal with unexpected circumstances and rise above adversity. You need to be constantly aware of new situations and when your sense of direction is clear, it is easier to make good decisions in ad-hoc situations.

Commitment

Once we embark on an important enterprise, success requires willingness to persevere in the face of difficulties and challenges.

Enthusiastic faith

Successful leaders believe strongly in their mission, and their enthusiasm is contagious. How do you inspire other people?

Compassion

You need to remain sensitive to the needs of people around you. We must strive to protect the best interests of those working with us.

Staying power

The adage reminds us: "It is not how you start, but how you finish." But also remember that if you have started something stupid, it is better to stop doing it rather than finish it with force.

Service to others

Self-centred leaders generally have short tenures. The leader devoted to serving others, helping them to reach their goals, is the one that finds eager followers. Do you add value to others?

Summary

What if you built these qualities into your life and really started to invest in yourself and add value to others? What would change?

Here are some reflective questions you can ask yourself to promote your thinking:

- Do you have a clear sense of direction?
- Have you made your own personal mission statement?
- Do you have yearly and monthly plans on how to achieve your goals?
- Are you able to see the big picture? How could you improve on this?
- Are you committed to your goals?
- Do you procrastinate?
- How do you inspire other people?
- How do you inspire yourself?
- How could you connect with people better?
- Are you a servant leader?

Write down your own thoughts here:

WEEK 39: WHAT CHANGE STRATEGIES ARE AVAILABLE AND HOW ARE THEY DEPLOYED?

Change strategies are not a new discussion topic, but they still keep people talking about the most effective change strategies available and how they are best deployed. Thurley and Wirdenius identified some key advantages and disadvantages of change management in 1973, which was later summarised by Lockitt and 3T Productions Ltd. (2004) in the figure below.

Change Management Strategies

Strategy	Advantages	Disadvantages
Directive	Relatively fast	Ignores the views of those affected by change.
Expert	Use relevant expertise. Small groups required. Relatively fast to implement	Expertise may be challenged. Resistance of those not consulted
Negotiated	Change recipients have some say. Resistance to change likely to be reduced (or areas of disagreement highlighted)	May be relatively slow. Anticipated change may have to be modified
Educative	People committed to change	Relatively slow. Likely to require more resources and more costs involved
Participative	Change more likely to be accepted. More people committed to change. More opportunity	Relatively slow to implement. More complex to manage. Will require more resources. Increased costs

FAST
Clearly Planned
Little Involvement
Need to overcome resistance

SLOW
Exploratory
Wide Involvement
Minimise Resistance

Directive change strategy

This strategy highlights the manager's right to manage change and the use of authority to impose change with little or no involvement of other people. This approach may lead to valuable information and ideas being missed and there is usually strong resentment from staff when changes are imposed rather than discussed and agreed.

Expert change strategy

This approach sees the management of change as a problem-solving process that needs to be resolved by an 'expert'. This approach is usually applicable to more technical problems and will most often be led by a specialist project team or senior manager. There is likely to be little involvement from those affected by the change.

Negotiating change strategy

This approach highlights the willingness on the part of senior managers to negotiate and bargain in order to affect change. Senior managers must also accept that adjustments and concessions may need to be made in order to implement change. This approach acknowledges that those affected by change have the right to have a say in what changes are made, how they are implemented, and the expected outcomes.

Educative change strategy

This approach involves changing people's values and beliefs in order for them to fully support the changes being made and move toward the development of a shared set of organisational values that individuals are willing and able to support. A mixture of activities will be used: education, persuasion, training and selection, all led by consultants, specialists and in-house experts.

Participative change strategy

This strategy stresses the full involvement of all of those involved in, and affected by, the anticipated changes. Although driven by senior managers, the process will be less management-dominated and driven more by groups or individuals within the organisation. The views of all involved will be taken into account before changes are made. Outside consultants and experts can be used to facilitate the process but they will not make any decisions as to the outcomes.

Which one is the best and how is that change strategy deployed?

Summary

Well, you might want to ask yourself: which advantages and disadvantages do you want to have? It is quite clear that in this imperfect world there is no perfect change strategy available. However, the participant change strategy seems quite compelling, especially because some of the disadvantages found by Thurley and Wirdenius can be overcome with the latest methods such as the Customer Experience Innovation Method. The benefits of this approach are that any changes made are more likely to be supported due to the involvement of all those affected; the commitment of individuals and groups within the organisation will increase as those individuals and groups feel ownership over the changes being implemented. The organisation and individuals also have the opportunity to learn from this experience and will know more about the organisation and how it functions, thus increasing their skills, knowledge and effectiveness within the organisation.

Here are some reflective questions you can ask yourself to promote your thinking:

- Does your organisation have clearly defined change management strategies? How would they help to foster change?
- Which of the change strategies described above are you using?
- Which strategy would be most suitable for your current situation?
- How could you alleviate change resistance in your organisation?
- Are you personally against or for change, for the most part?

Write down your own thoughts here:

WEEK 40: WHAT KIND OF MANAGEMENT ENSURES SUCCESS IN BPM?

Based on my scientific research, I have found the following capabilities related to management and leadership to be necessary for an organisation to succeed in Business Process Management (BPM) initiatives. Have you ever spent time to think about how your management practices affect the work done in the organisation? Below you can find most relevant capabilities contributing to your organisation's success.

Managers share vision and information with their subordinates

It is important for employees to know where the organisation is heading. In previous times, hiding information was quite normal, but nowadays all the information is available for everyone anyway, so there is no reason for managers not to share it with their employees.

Managers place confidence between supervisors and their subordinates

In many organisations, middle management is the biggest obstacle to success. Higher lever managers do not trust their middle management and middle management do not trust their subordinates. This causes several bottlenecks that hinder communication and cooperation. Confidence between these parties is crucial.

Managers constructively use their subordinates' ideas

Those people who actually do the work are the ones that have good ideas about how to improve organisation. Thus, managers should listen to their employees and use the ideas to improve the organisation.

Top management generally has realistic expectations of the projects

Top management is often a little bit disconnected from realistic expectations. According to Bain & Company, 80% of CEOs think that their organisation is providing great customer experience and only 8% of their customers agree. Top management should understand what expectations exists towards the improvement projects.

Top management has sufficient knowledge about the projects

Top management should know what kind of improvement projects are going on in the organisation. This helps them to understand what is going on and how it fits into the bigger picture. Therefore, it is important to make sure that the top management stays up-to-date about your improvement projects.

Top management frequently communicates with the project team and users

Managers who do not talk to their employees are bad managers. They should not sit in their ivory towers and give orders; they should participate and communicate with everyone in the organisation. That helps the flow of information and stops the bottlenecks developing.

Top management generally supports changes in processes

If there is no support for changes by top management, those improvements will not have the chance to be realised. The organisation should have a culture of continuous improvement and top management should support all good changes.

The organisation has an empowered process owner who takes responsibility

Someone should be responsible for the processes in your organisation. That person needs to be empowered to optimise the process and he should also have appropriate education and knowledge to do that.

The performance measurements adequately correspond to the processes and changes

You get what you measure. Thus, your organisation should only measure what is really important and when you get the results, you should implement the changes as required. There is no point in measuring if you do not act. The customer experience is the process and the organisation should carefully measure their performance based on factors related to that.

The employees are empowered to make decisions

An old-fashioned perspective of management believes that managers know everything and should tell employees what to do. However, we are all people who are capable of thinking and we should be allowed to use our brains for the benefit of the organisation. Managers do not need to decide every little detail and employees should be empowered to make decisions that take the organisation forward.

Summary

Everything rises and falls with leadership. So, make sure that your management practices are in order. Remember to communicate well and keep the employees in the loop. Build trust in all levels of organisations and deal with matters promptly, using the inputs you receive from different directions. Do reality checks on the projects and make sure they stay within schedule and budget.

You can reflect on these factors in relation to your organisation: for example, with following questions:

- How open is the communication that you have in your organisation?
- How is the confidence between your different management levels and their subordinates?
- Does your organisation listen to ideas and actually implement them to improve the organisation?
- Does your top management have realistic expectations for projects?
- Does your top management support changes in processes?
- Do you measure the right things and act based on the results?
- Are your employees empowered to make decisions?

Write down your own thoughts here:

WEEK 41: HOW CAN YOU BECOME A COACHING LEADER?

Would you like to be a leader who is able to help employees become more effective and enjoy their work more? Leaders who master coaching skills add value to their organisations by adding value to their people. As we all know, no matter what your organisation does, employees generate successful customer outcomes by creating products or providing services, so giving them proper assistance adds more value to your organisation.

To be a coaching leader, you need determination, integrity and courage. By embracing listening and learning skills, and considering what really matters in your life, you can successfully coach people. You need to set an example by always telling the truth and holding yourself accountable. To remain competitive, you need to create a learning culture and enhance your own skills too. The following paragraphs outline some skills that you can learn to become a coaching leader:

Be an exemplary leader

Employees watch you all the time and they will believe what you do more than what you say. That means the old saying of "Do as I say, not as I do" is false. When you enforce your words with consistent actions, they are much more powerful. In this context, "therefore all things whatsoever ye would that men should do to you, do ye even so to them" works really well (Matthew 7:12 KJV). Employees will adopt your message if your behaviour is exemplary, constructive, and you demonstrate strong discipline to inspire trust between people.

Have great communication skills

As a coaching leader, you need really good communication skills. To lead others, do not talk at them. Instead, communicate with them on a deeper level. Learn to listen and understand the meaning of what they are saying, and then speak in a constructive way. You should find yourself listening more than talking. If you feel that you need better skills in communication, you can participate in coaching training.

Take advice from other people

Help your employees remain open to your thoughts by listening to their advice and changing in response to it. If other people present good ideas, use them and give credit as appropriate. Do not be afraid to change your mind, if new information or actions make that the sensible option. Taking advice from others is not a sign of weakness, but a sign of mutual respect. Good leaders surround themselves with people who compensate for their weaknesses.

Search for causes

Look beyond the surface that people present to you. Just like in Business Process Management, to investigate beyond superficial effects to understand any fundamental causes, you have to look within people, their true motivations and even their fears, in order to coach them. If you only work with the effects, you will never be a good coaching leader.

Follow disciplined priorities and schedules

Demonstrate the ability to manage your actions and set an example for others to control theirs. Prioritise everything and focus only on things that matter. You cannot manage time (it goes forward no matter what you do), so manage what you do with it.

Be a vision-oriented leader

At times, work can be repetitive and monotonous if employees only focus on the actual tasks they do. When you show people how their tasks fit into a larger picture, they are able to see the contribution they make to something more meaningful. Organisations exist to produce successful customer outcomes and everyone should understand their purpose in that overall process. A coaching leader with vision can help people to see that.

Give appraisals generously

Honest appraisals cost little and yield a great return. Some people would actually favour a proper thank you from their manager over a small monetary bonus. I suggest giving appraisals publicly and constructive feedback privately. Avoid using e-mail, unless it is the best communication medium at that moment for some justified reason. Know what your people do well and praise them for that.

Summary

Coaching leaders help employees to enhance their skills and develop a clear sense of purpose. That will help people to be productive. You can never be perfect and therefore you need to be an honest coaching leader by practising what you preach. Genuinely serve others rather than insisting on being served. Use your employees' time efficiently and carefully by displaying sincere appreciation for what they do. All of the skills previously mentioned are limitless, so you can always become better at them. However, remember to focus on what is useful and important.

Here are some reflective questions you can ask yourself to promote your thinking:

- Do you keep your promises?
- Do you give feedback in a constructive way? And privately?
- Do you appraise people for their accomplishments?
- Do you focus on causes rather than effects?
- Do you prioritise what you do?
- Do you help people to see the bigger picture?
- Do you prefer face-to-face contact to e-mail?

Write down your own thoughts here:

WEEK 42: UNDERSTANDING YOUR CUSTOMERS THROUGH RESEARCH

Does your organisation use market research as a method for understanding your customers? If yes, how well has it served you? If your organisation does not carry out market research, then you have saved your money, because often market research is not able to produce the results that help your business to succeed. The reason for this is that market research focuses on conscious choices of customers, not the unconscious ones that really drive their purchase behaviour. This can easily lead to a situation where your organisation produces services or products that, according to market research, your customers wanted, but ultimately do not buy them. However, this does not free you from understanding your customers and how to serve them better.

Testing your new products or services can be tricky. If you conduct live testing with whatever you want to offer to your customers, you may get inaccurate or misleading results. Some people may claim they like new services or products, but they tend to go back to their old ways. Furthermore, market research participants may say that they are willing to try something new because, under research circumstances, no risk is involved. However, in real life with their own money, they would not take that risk. The unconscious mind of people prefers to be risk-averse and for these reasons, you get inaccurate results from your market research.

Asking people about your products or services does not produce the most accurate and appropriate results. When people know that they are observed or surveyed, they will respond in unnatural ways. They think about what answers you would like to hear and their behaviour changes to the way they think you want them to behave. Therefore, traditional interviews and survey market research cannot give natural and unbiased answers. A better solution is to use observation of your customers' behaviour rather than asking them about it. Watching how people behave allows you to see the unconscious and the conscious minds working together. To get this information, it requires undercover observation of your customers. Try to get indirect information as much as possible, without people noticing. Just remember to be ethical and obey the local laws. Record how long people spend with your product or service, how often they touch them, whether they seem to enjoy their time with your business, whether they recommend your services to others, etc. There are several ways to observe and measure people in an ethical way so that you still receive useful information about your business.

Compared to traditional market research methodologies, you can get better results to understand customer behaviour by taking human psychology into account. For example, you can use the AFECT criteria (by Graves, 2010), discussed in the coming paragraphs, which assess these factors for market research reports.

Analysis of behavioural data

Ask for a report that explains how your customers conduct themselves. The best reports take actual behaviours and sales information into account, and do not just ask customers for conscious opinions. The key is to understand how you can fulfil the real needs of your customers based on their unconscious minds. Analysing current behavioural data helps you to make predictions about their future behaviour.

Frame of mind

When customers are out of their normal buying environment and know they are being observed, they are also in the wrong frame of mind to provide on-target answers about what they are really feeling. Do your best not to change the frame of mind when you are doing a study to understand your customers by keeping the environment of market research as natural as possible.

Environment

The study should be conducted in the appropriate customer environment, not in a sterile focus-group room or away from the situations in which customers will be making their actual buying decisions. The best place to observe your customers is in their natural habitat. In some cases that may be difficult to do, but with new technologies it is getting easier all the time.

Covert study

Knowing that they are being studied influences customers' answers to unfavourable direction. If you can, let them think that your questions are exploring something else altogether. Do not ask something if you really do not have to. However, do be careful not to go overboard being covert; keep ethical rules and laws in mind.

Timeframe

Customers' unconscious minds make decisions quickly. Therefore, favour quick replies over long questions that require time to answer. If the study you are conducting is not beneficial to your customers, it will not be beneficial to you either; so make their time count. People appreciate your business more when you appreciate their time.

Summary

You need to move forward from traditional market research methods, as they may not serve you well enough. Live testing your services or products, using the AFECT criteria, and being aware of the relationship between your customers' conscious and unconscious minds will help you to improve your understanding and ability to predict their buying behaviour. Your ultimate goal in conducting market research should be to understand how you could better fulfil your customers' needs.

Here are some reflective questions you can ask yourself to promote your thinking:

- What is the most important question that you need an answer for that market research could provide?
- Has your previous market research actually helped you to understand your customers better?
- Is your organisation taking people's unconscious mind into account when conducting market researches?
- Do you conduct live testing of your products or services with real customers in as natural environment as possible?

Write down your own thoughts here:

WEEK 43: USING METRICS TO BUILD CUSTOMER LOYALTY

Measuring and analysing customer loyalty is important for any organisation. Many organisations spend a lot of money on Customer Relationship Management (CRM) systems and the like. They use it to automate customer account management and to collect and store customer data for marketing and sales purposes. You can accomplish most of the necessary steps without expensive CRM software, and no CRM system will help if it is used in the wrong way. Customer loyalty building is a network of relationships, not a predictable formula, although you do need metrics to succeed. Your customer relationship management metrics and analytics should cover these categories of measurements to be more meaningful.

Prerequisites

It all starts from your organisation's reason to exist. To justify its existence, you need to measure the prerequisites such as customer needs and successful customer outcomes. This will be by far the hardest to measure, but at the same time it is also the most important. You have a thorough understanding of what customers really need from your organisation and how you can deliver successful outcomes to them. Expensive CRM systems or traditional market research methods cannot help you with that.

Inputs

Your organisation needs new customers and you can measure their acquisition by tracking leads, proposals, bids and sales processes. New customers are the inputs that you are going to turn into loyal customers later; make sure that you have new customers in the pipeline at all times. At the same time you have to maintain your existing customers. This is not something that you need CRM for; what you need is sales people who actually care about the customers. To build customer loyalty, everyone in your organisation has to understand the price of customer acquisition to value existing customers.

Processes

When you design metrics for processes, measure actions that strengthen your customer relationships. You can ask the question: "Is this helping my customers to succeed?" for every performance indicator that you have in your process metrics. If something is not contributing towards successful customer outcomes, then do not do or measure that. Often, process metrics in organisations do not hold any measures for customer loyalty; luckily, you know better not to make the same mistake.

Outputs

Outputs are different from outcomes. They are ways to produce outcomes. When you design metrics for outputs, keep the intended outcomes in mind all the time. You can measure such countable things as new orders, orders processed, samples or demos provided, bids submitted, phone calls placed by your sales team, and customers visited. Do not get blinded by numbers though: more is not always better. A person who makes five calls and makes three deals is more effective than one who makes 10 calls and closes four deals. Design the output metrics so that they help you to pinpoint the problems in processes that are not able to produce the outcomes that your customer seeks.

Outcomes

Successful customer outcomes are the most important metrics that you have. For an organisation's internal purposes you can track gross margin, profitability, gross revenues, marketing ROI, net income, and the effectiveness of supplier relations and other partnerships. However, to thrive in the competitive business world, you have to measure the outcomes that lead to high customer loyalty. These metrics include, for example, customers' recommendations of your services or products to their friends. Another important indicator may be that will they use your services or buy your products again. These two outcome metrics tell a lot more about customer loyalty than traditional organisational centric metrics than most CRM systems offer.

Summary

Analysing metrics can help you to build customer loyalty. To be successful in that, you need to look at your metrics from a new perspective, measuring those aspects that matter for your customer. You have to revisit your performance indicators on prerequisites, inputs, processes, outputs and outcomes to evaluate which ones are helping to build customer loyalty. CRM systems are not bad in themselves, but they are often used in a non-productive way to get metrics that do not help to achieve the appropriate end goal.

Here are some reflective questions you can ask yourself to promote your thinking:
- Have you evaluated your performance indicators from a customer loyalty perspective?
- How many of your metrics actually deal with customer loyalty?

- Do you have an over-complicated CRM system, which people do not use to its full potential?
- Does everyone in your organisation know the price of customer acquisition?
- Have you carefully analysed the customer needs and successful outcomes?
- Do you measure and analyse how your organisation is performing in terms of producing successful customer outcomes?
- Does your CRM system help your sales people to do what they are supposed to do?
- Does your CRM system increase or decrease customer loyalty?

Write down your own thoughts here:

WEEK 44: HOW CAN I PROVIDE GREAT EMPLOYEE EXPERIENCES?

There is a lot of talk out there about providing great customer experiences, but besides customers, we also have to think about those people who provide those customer experiences—your employees. You want to hold on to your star players and develop those who are not yet able to live up to the standards you have set for your organisation.

In supporting your employees, you can start with the basics: that is providing the tools and materials they need. It is also in the employer's interests to give employees good tools that they like to use, because they will work more efficiently. To create a great employee experience, build a successful, committed team and help them to connect tasks to purpose by explaining how their jobs support the organisation and its goals (in creating successful customer outcomes). Sincere, genuine and frequent praise is a powerful, cost-effective employee development tool. Some employees would actually prefer compliments from their boss over a small monetary bonus. You should seek employees' opinions and actively listen to them. To be a great leader, you need to support your employees instead of misusing them. Here are some ideas on how to provide great employee experience in your organisation.

Give everyone an opportunity to shine

When an employee is doing his job well and enjoys performing and meeting the needs of the organisation, it is the best situation for a great employee experience. Leaders are responsible for aligning employees' tasks with work they are good at and then helping their positions grow and develop into tasks they might not even realise they can do well. Organisations sometimes place good people in jobs that are wrong for them. Recognise this kind of situation and redirect misplaced employees so they can shine elsewhere or do something else. Take measures before they hurt the organisation or the employees lose their confidence and poison the work atmosphere. Whether the person needs training or reassignment, handle such steps as opportunities to grow, not as the results of failure.

Everyone should know his or her part within the organisation

Employees want to know what they are supposed to do to accomplish their part in the provision of successful customer outcomes. A job description alone does not ensure that an employee will perform well and understand his or her role in the organisation. As a leader, you need to coordinate with your employees to make sure that you and they understand their work's full implications, how their work connects to results and what to do when deviations occur in business processes. Providing good results consistently means performing well under varying and sometimes unpredictable conditions. And as you know, great leaders enable their people to feel proud and empowered about what they do. Their leadership helps employees connect with their colleagues and their organisation.

Respect employees' opinions

Employees will cease to contribute if they believe that their opinions do not matter. Do not wait for them to push into your field of vision if you are not sensitive enough to hear them. Why? For two very good reasons: to get the full benefits each employee can provide and to improve your business processes through professional opinion. Ask for their opinions about processes, the organisation and your leadership. You do not have to agree with them, but do not disrespect them either. Simply by acknowledging them, and demonstrating that you truly hear and understand what they are saying, you give them powerful affirmation. First seek to understand and then to be understood. By doing that, your employees are more likely to give you ideas and information you can use to improve your organisation's performance in providing successful customer outcomes.

Employees are committed to quality work together

Customers are everyone's business, so do not be satisfied teaching employees solely how to perform their tasks within the processes. To make each employee's work more meaningful, demonstrate how it connects to the successful customer outcomes that your organisation produces. Employees who understand that their poor performance in quality could compromise another important part of the process will perform their jobs better. They will not wait passively until someone else fixes a problem; they will contact someone who can fix it. Great process teams know what they are doing and how to do it best. In that kind of team, members support each other and coordinate their tasks, bond and recognise each other's contributions. As a leader, keep your employees committed by helping them to stay focused on their success rather than on any disruptive events. If possible, you may even ask your customers to give appraisals to your employees.

Treat employees as individuals

Great leaders know that people are not machines and should not be treated as objects. Even though Henry Ford cynically said that he had to hire a whole person to get the pair of hands he wanted, you know better that getting the full power of each employee's passion and creativity is much more valuable than just hiring someone who merely fulfils required tasks (you can automate those parts of the processes). Employee satisfaction and performance increases when they know that colleagues care about them and have a genuine interest in their lives. No matter how hard you try, you cannot force great work out of people that you mistreat. And your organisation cannot compete if your employees only provide perfunctory performances. They must bring their heart to work. To nurture their networking and involvement, create an environment that recognises that real people have lives outside of work. When employees feel that their employers respect their dignity, they work harder and bring more to the table than you had asked for initially.

Create opportunities to grow and learn

Most of your employees (but not all) like to grow and learn new things throughout their lives. You may not know that, because many employees will avoid taking risks if they believe that the organisation will punish them for even the smallest failures when trying. But there is no growth without pain; people need to leave their comfort zones to learn new things. To receive the benefits that come from helping employees to improve, create an organisational environment that supports risk-taking and the inevitable failures that accompany it. Support your employees in learning new needed skills and securing educational opportunities. Each person should become familiar with several tasks within the process scope so the group has coverage during absences or transitions also. Employees will trust and appreciate you more as their leader if they know you will help them advance and not hold them back for selfish reasons. Be ready for change due to the growth you encouraged rather than trying to stunt growth in order to prevent change, because the fact is that you cannot prevent it.

Summary

Many managers, CEOs, leaders and so on say employees are their organisation's greatest assets (have you heard that one before?). This gesture is too often meaningless because these executives' actions contradict their words. Some research findings show that the leaders who elicit the most out of their employees are those who give their employees the most—and that is not necessarily in terms of salary, but in respect, dignity, and support. The leaders who derive the best financial performances from their employees are the ones who are the least motivated by money. If you work hard for your people, they will work hard for you; ultimately, everyone will benefit. You can use the ideas described here to start the path of growth and learning in your organisation to produce successful customer outcomes through great employee experiences.

Here are some reflective questions you can ask yourself to promote your thinking:

- Do you give genuine appraisals to your employees?
- What could you change to improve the support of growth and learning in your organisation?
- Does your organisation treat employees as individuals?
- Are colleagues also friends in your organisation?
- Is the customer everybody's business in your organisation?
- Do you objectify employees?
- Why do people ask for salary increases in your organisation?
- What are your employees lacking in skills or knowledge?
- Do you provide a great employee experience?

Write down your own thoughts here:

WEEK 45: HOW CAN I BECOME A BETTER PERSON?

We all ask that question at some point of our life. There are probably no right answers to this question, but presented within this week's entry are some ideas for you to use as a tool to develop yourself.

Embrace the current time and place

Accept your current situation and make peace with it. There is nothing to gain from complaining or worrying over your current situation. Too many people are stuck in the past or constantly live in the future. Neither of those perspectives is very helpful. You have to use the past events as learning experiences and naturally you need to plan your future, but everything happens right now and therefore your actions and decisions at this very moment shape what is to come. Therefore, embrace the time and place where you are right now and make the best of it.

Keep moving forward

You cannot go backwards; time is set to move forward at all times (even if it may not always feel like that). The only thing you have power over is the present time. So do not let your past failures undermine your today—and through your today, your future. As John C. Maxwell says in his book cover: "Today Matters" (ISBN 1931722528). If you want to become something else tomorrow, you need to work on it today. You have to change your way of thinking by engaging the thoughts that support the pattern you want to develop. Do not let yourself become stagnant and mediocre; there are already enough people like that in this world. Do not merely settle for what you have, believing that there is nothing better that you can gain. Instead, try to improve mentally, spiritually and physically every day. You need to actively resist life's constraints and other people's negativity and aim for new levels in your skills, career and relationships by moving forward.

Develop better transformational relationships

Work on your relationships every day. Just as other people can bring out your best, you can help others to reach their full potential. Seek to develop better transformational relationships. That may be challenging in these social media networking times, but you can use those tools to your benefit. Instead of quantity, focus on the quality of your network. Your relationships with your colleagues, family and friends are the most important things in your life. To keep them healthy, eliminate strife from your relationships with others. Make compromises and focus only on important aspects. Learn to love people and accept them with their imperfections; you are not perfect either.

Your relationships are so-called emotional bank accounts. You make withdrawals when you behave selfishly or break commitments, as examples. You make deposits by overlooking mistakes and being generous with compliments, encouragement and support. Give freely your consideration and assistance without expecting something in return. Seek to make more deposits than withdrawals from your emotional bank accounts with others.

Be positive and choose to be happy

Did you know that you can actually decide to be happy? If you do so, it will significantly make you happier each day. We as human beings are subject to our own thoughts, thus changing them will take us forward. Just as you must change your thinking to enact positive change, you must realign your words also. Negative words and thoughts will keep you from reaching true happiness. Many negative thought patterns originate in childhood and to break free from them and reprogram your mind: for example, learn NLP, talk to a therapist, get coaching, etc. You can actually create your own happiness.

Develop better habits and ways of thinking

Humans are creatures of habit with fixed ways of thinking. Your habits determine your daily behaviour: when you wake up, what you eat, what you do and how you think. To change your life, first identify your bad habits. If you make the decision to do so, you can actually break these negative patterns that hold you back. Once you have made the conscious choice to develop better habits, practise the change every day. It will take you out of your comfort zone, but just keep on moving forward. Once the new habit takes root, it will become much easier. In some cases you may also want to get professional coaching to help identify your bad habits and to develop ways to get rid of them.

Stay passionate about your work and life

Life can wear you down through constant trials and disappointments. Instead, it is more useful to focus on what is good in your work, life and in this world. Your positive attitude is contagious and can inspire everyone around you, including yourself. Set meaningful goals for your life and pursue them eagerly. Learn to know yourself and what you like. Writing a personal mission statement and then following it will help you stay passionate about your work and life.

Summary

Becoming a better person depends a lot on you. You may want to partake in some self-reflection to identify the parts of your life that you are least satisfied with. Then you can develop a plan to start becoming a better you step by step. Remember to be connected to this moment and focus your thoughts in a more fruitful direction. You can also increase your own happiness by just deciding every morning to be happy for that day. It may also be useful to identify some of your bad habits and start to reprogram your thoughts into more useful ways of thinking.

Here are some reflective questions you can ask yourself to promote your thinking:

- How happy are you each day?
- Have you decided to be happy?
- How could you improve your life?
- What you are not happy with in your life?
- Are you passionate about what you do for a living?
- Do you put more effort into the quality of your relationships rather than the quantity?
- Do you tend to dwell on the past?

Write down your own thoughts here:

WEEK 46: HOW CAN EMPOWERMENT HELP YOU TO GET MORE CUSTOMERS?

Empowering your employees and customers in the right way does not only help your organisation to get new customers, but also serve your existing ones better. As we all know, an organisation itself is not a living thing and as such cannot do anything. It is the individuals within an organisation that will produce the successful customer outcomes that your organisation wishes to provide. By empowering both your employees and customers, you can get more business coming your way.

Empowering your employees

Technology advances really fast nowadays and people are using their mobile devices throughout the day. That gives your employees the potential to engage in discussions with your new potential customers, as well as help them to serve existing ones better. It also enables your customers to interact with your organisation regardless of your business times (self-service, on-line discussions, social media, and so on). That has implications on how your organisation should handle its social media accounts and such. Empowering your employees to have discussions with customers will help your organisation to serve customers better. But of course there has to be rules on how that is done to minimise the risk to the organisation. Still, one should bear in mind that people will have those discussions anyway (you cannot really prevent that), so why not support it in a fruitful and productive way?

On-line interactions used to be text- and image-based for a long time, but since video services (for example, YouTube and Vimeo) became popular and everyone started to have webcams on their laptops, audio-visual communication has become important. You can harness this trend by using the videos as a medium for distributing your message. Your employees can share information and show their expertise through videos and that may appeal to new customers. Video is also a very convenient way to serve your current customers by sharing tutorials, how-to videos and so on.

Social media networks are important for managing an organisation's brand value. As you already know, your employees are using Facebook, LinkedIn, Wikipedia, instant messaging, and many other social media tools and technologies each day. Many of them actually know how to use those tools to benefit your organisation. Do not punish them for such grassroots initiatives, but empower employees to be proactive problem solvers for your customers. In the end, that serves both sides.

Empowering your customers

To be able to empower your customers, you need to make excellent services or products a priority. You have to enable your employees to engage and assist customers on Facebook, YouTube and similar social media sites. They can help the customers faster and more personally that way. At the same time, you need to keep successful customer outcomes and excellent customer experience in mind. Even though social media may be a more relaxed communication medium than, for example, official business meetings, the code of conduct for relationships is still in order. That way your customers can spread their good experiences easier (so long as you provide them).

Nowadays, mobile browsing and mobile applications enable everyone to have a vast amount of information at their fingertips. You should focus on mass influencers, who are almost twice as likely to use the mobile web as other customers. To earn the respect of these certain customers and other mobile users, your organisation should empower them with mobile offers, information and customer service. You need to be where they are and that is in their iPhones, BlackBerrys and such.

To empower customers to work for you, strengthen word of mouth about your organisation by building a loyal following. This will take some time and continuous effort. What you want to do is to turn your most influential customers into evangelists who will promote your organisation on-line (and receive free advertising!). To do that, you need to locate the web users who like your organisation the most and then find a way to enhance the impact they have on their on-line peers.

Summary

Empowering both your employees and customers together may help your organisation to touch base with new and existing customers on a new level. People will be using social media sites and other new communication mediums anyway, so it is better to use them for the organisation's benefit. Using these new ways to communicate will require your organisation to change its attitude towards social media and to develop protocols for using those tools to the benefit of the organisation.

Here are some reflective questions you can ask yourself to promote your thinking:
- Has your organisation empowered its employees to engage with customers?
- What do customers say about you on the Internet?
- Is your organisation's plan for social media up-to-date?

- Do your customers work for your benefit (by recommending your services or products to others)?

Write down your own thoughts here:

WEEK 47: HOW CAN YOU LEARN TO LISTEN ACTIVELY AND GET BETTER RESULTS WITH OTHERS?

Active listening is said to be one of the most important skills that leaders can have. Active listening can help you to find other people's motives, desires, and understanding to seek common ground to work on. Many problems could be easily avoided just by listening more. Old command and conquer times of management are behind us and leading through influence is found to be more efficient. Nowadays, you can get through to people by getting them to buy into your ideas. Furthermore, handling difficult situations becomes much easier through listening.

The following are some ideas on how you can use active listening as a tool to influence (notice this is not manipulation; your goal has to be to seek common ground, not to manipulate) other people.

Do not react immediately

One of the most common mistakes is to react immediately to what another person says. Have you noticed how your tension level rises when you are cross? Often we say whatever comes into our mind first; however, that is not a very fruitful way to act. It is better to count to 10 and let the first wave go over you. Then you get your emotions under control and you can start to think again. You will be in control again and you can actively listen to the other person and what he or she is actually saying (the meanings behind the words).

Focus on the other person

Make your goal to be more interested in what the other person says rather than saying something interesting. For you to be able to say something meaningful to the other person, you must first understand what the other person is telling you. Let the other person dominate the conversation and carefully choose when you engage. Often, it takes people some time to get to the actual point and if you interrupt them too early you might not hear the part that was actually important. If you do not understand what the other person says or means, then actively ask more detailed questions.

Help the other person to engage with you

If the other person is agitated, busy or otherwise not in the best mind-set, help them to get to a better place both emotionally and physically. Let them vent if that is needed, warm them up if they are cold (either mentally or physically), and help them to start a meaningful discussion. Do not let first impressions of people fool you.

Next, once you and the counterpart are at the appropriate emotional stage, there is an opportunity to start to move the discussion forward and influence how others perceive things. We all have our own agendas and most of the matters in this world are some kind of compromise between different desires. There are many simple ways to influence people toward the direction that you think is the right way to go. Still, keep in mind that manipulation is not beneficial to anyone (not even to you). The following paragraphs contain a few ideas you can try out this week.

Turning discouragement around

For some reason, people usually like to discourage others more than encourage. When you present ideas and get comments like: "Are you sure that is the right thing to do?" or something similar, that is a good opportunity to use Dave Hibbard's impossibility question: "What is something that would be impossible to do, but if you could do it, would dramatically influence your success?" Naturally, you may have to change the question to suit your situation, but I am sure you get the idea. What you want to do is to change the other person's reaction: from resisting your idea to bouncing around other possibilities to realise what you have proposed. This way you end up either having the other person agree with you or with an even better idea than the original one.

Move from a superficial level to a deeper level

People like to stick to a superficial level of discussion. This is a great opportunity to listen to others in a deeper way and use that information to engage them in a discussion that is more meaningful. Ask them questions that are related to your discussion topic; make them pause, reflect and reveal something more than is immediately evident. Examples of good questions to get the other people to think about could be: "When you say...what do you mean by it?", "What could be done to change the situation?", "How important is this to you?", and so on. What you what them to do is to pause and notice that the question you presented to them was not trivial. That way they start to see more value in discussing it with you and you can use your listening skills to get the bottom of the matters.

Show appreciation and humbleness

Care for other people. Try to listen to them to understand their viewpoint and then move people to where you want them to be. Show them appreciation in concrete ways. Saying thanks is nice, but in many cases you can probably do more. Always take the extra step; others will appreciate you for that. Be humble and give others space to act. If you make a mistake, admit it, remit it and apologise. Saying thanks and apologising does not do you much good unless you change the situation so that it is unlikely for the same mistake to happen again.

Summary

Active listening is a skill that is essential for success in life. There is so much noise in the world that too few people stop to listen to others. The ones that do are noted and appreciated. To listen to others better, you should not react immediately. What you should do is focus on the other person and help the other person to engage with you. Of course there is much more you can do, but with these steps you can get started with immediate results.
Once you are able to listen to others, you can start influencing them in a positive way. Through influence you can, for example, turn discouragement around. To start influencing others, you can move from a superficial level to a deeper level of discussion and show appreciation and humbleness more.

Here are some reflective questions you can ask yourself to promote your thinking:

- Do you get discouraged often?
- How do you react when someone confronts you?
- Do you consider yourself a humble person?
- Do others perceive you as a person who appreciates others?
- Do you focus more on talking than listening?
- How could you listen to others better?
- How could you relate to others better?

Write down your own thoughts here:

WEEK 48: ARE YOU PRODUCING MORE MOMENTS OF MAGIC THAN MISERY FOR YOUR CUSTOMERS?

Jan Carlson, the former CEO of SAS in the 1980s, defined moments of truth as interactions that any organisation has with their customers throughout the day. He estimated that every single person might have up to 50,000 moments of truth in their lives every day. We can take this concept even further and say that all of these moments are either moments of magic or moments of misery. Positive customer interactions (moments of magic) aim to delight, pleasure and create rapport. Those moments of magic enforce the customer relationship. Organisations who actively intend to create moments of magic create that rapport through memorable, personal and useful interactions. Their goal is to make customers' lives easier, simpler and more successful.

It is important to remember that any moment of truth can go wrong. In that case it turns into a moment of misery. It will weaken the customer relationship and decrease the change of success in the future. These moments can include when a customer service assistant says something snappy, sells a broken product, does not greet the customer properly, or any other situation where the customer interaction is not ideal. The traditional marketing education says that the more customer interactions the better, but actually this concept of moments of misery proves it to be the other way around. If you are not sure that you will create a moment of magic, then it is better not to have that customer interaction at all. A good example of this situation is when Bentley used to send out text messages to new car owners to let them know what manufacturing phase their car was in. They thought that customers would like to know what's going on with their car. But the customers actually thought: "Instead of sending these messages, why don't you build my car?". Of course it was automated, but for customers these extra interactions were moments of misery rather than magic, and consequently Bentley stopped sending the text messages.

You can purposefully design moments of magic into your business. It requires you to put yourself into your customers' shoes and think about everything you do from their perspective. Your business processes are the way you create moments of magic. The environment is where you do it and the delivery is the actual situation where it is produced to the customer. You need to have additional consideration for each of these settings to create an overall moment of magic.

Environment

This is the place where you deliver the moment of magic through your processes. Depending on your business, it can vary greatly. In some cases, it is a cornerstone shop, on-line class, public place, shopping mall or any other environment which is the most optimal for your customers to receive your products or services. You can use the environment in a positive way to enhance your business. For example, if you have a restaurant, instead of cutting down all the trees, you could leave one big natural tree as a centrepiece and nurture it. Or if you have an artificial environment, such as a department store, you can simulate different layouts to find the optimal one for your customers. Nowadays you can even impress people via the Internet using graphical elements, increased accessibility and other ways that help to make the on-line experience a pleasant one.

Processes

Delivering moments of magic through your processes (how you do everything) requires solid understanding of customer needs and expectations. Most of the businesses focus on customer wants and are able to uncover a fraction of their needs. You can use such methods as the CEI (Customer Experience Innovation) Method to have an organised and effective way of identifying customer needs and aligning every process for delivering against them. What you need to do is to understand customer expectations, then deliver against them, and finally, manage those expectations. For example, a car sales man joking about cars breaking down would not create moments of magic unless the customer already knew this particular salesman to be a funny man.

Delivery

One frequently forgotten part of creating magic through delivery is handling the situations when something goes wrong. If you have built a good rapport with your customers through several moments of magic, they will find it easier to forgive you. When you deliver your products or services, you need to also focus on how it is done. There needs to be certain sensitivity towards the customer and what they are feeling. One size does not fit all, so your environment should be flexible (for example, people with disabilities and your processes should not see variance as the sole source of problems). Personalising the delivery in an appropriate way for the specific customer will create more magic.

Summary

Delivering moments of magic is essential for your business, since it helps you to build rapport with your customers. Each time you create a moment of magic, the customer relationship is strengthened and vice versa. You can create moments of magic by paying attention to the environment, processes, and delivery of your goods and services.

Here are some reflective questions you can ask yourself to promote your thinking:

- Have you evaluated whether, from your customers' perspective, the environment is optimal to receive your products or services?
- Are you using the business environment to create more moments of magic than misery?
- Have you used the natural elements of environment to support your business?
- If you have an on-line business, does your website impress the visitors or is it plain and dull?
- Have you identified what customers expect from your business?
- Are your business processes aligned to deliver against customer expectations?
- Do you deliver sloppy customer interactions or are they well-planned and rehearsed?
- Try to identify where, how and what do you deliver and what you could do to improve.

Write down your own thoughts here:

WEEK 49: ACTIVELY MANAGING TRANSITIONS

To start off this week, let's discuss the difference between transition and change: the latter is about those physical and emotional changes from one state to another. This could mean change an office to another place, changing from Windows to Mac or new members of a team. Transition is more of a psychological approach to working through the change (Bridges, 2003). Many organisations are good at making changes, but poor at managing transitions. And as is true with many things, trust is the most important building stone in transition. Leaders should be able to say what they do and do what they say. If this does not happen, then transition is going to be harder to manage.

Transition is funny in a way, since it starts with an end and ends with a start. The old must first die away, before the new can be born. The first stage of managing transition is to see an end to old ways. Then there is a neutral phase where the old is gone and the new is coming. The last phase is when the new is in use. To manage all three phases, you need truthfulness, clarity, consistency, and great communication. At the end of the day, actively managing transitions is all about helping employees to deal with uncertainty and fear that comes with changes that cause the transitions.

The end of an old era

The transition begins with the end of an old era. This is a very critical phase, because depending on how you manage the transition this will either lead back to the old ways or towards the new era with successful transition. Often, the ending of an old era is not handled actively, which may lead people to go back, because we are creatures of habit. To manage the end purposefully, you need to understand the change. Have a very clear plan for the change and what it is going to mean—specifically for all stakeholders. Do not focus on your old ways, but on new ways that you want to have in place. Ending something always means losing something. This may cause very strong emotions and resistance to change. Make the new era tempting. It is very important to have clear and open communication all the time and if something goes wrong during the change, don't hide it, just learn from it and you won't make the same mistake twice. Remember that the new era is the goal and work towards it.

The neutral era

This is the storm before the calm. In this neutral era, everything seems chaotic with some people still living in the old era and some in the new one. People are trying to readjust to new ways and they are giving up the old ways: for some people that is painful. However, not all of this is bad. It also creates space for creativity and cooperation. If you get people to work together, it will create an atmosphere where all the obstacles can be overcome together. It is like a romantic picture of a war where peace first ends, then people fight together to gain something and then peace comes again (true war is far from that in reality, but transition can be too). In this neutral phase, be ready to change the old rules. You may need to give people more slack to make the transition easier. Furthermore, you should keep your demands reasonable. It will take different people different lengths of time to adjust from old to new. Identify those people who find it easy and encourage them to support the others who find it difficult. Find sponsors who can work on your behalf. It is very important to make the goals for the new era very clear to everyone. People are able to navigate in chaos if the goals are clear and keeping those goals clear will require really good communication. All the concerns and issues need to be addressed and communicated properly.

The beginning of a new era

People do not like change because they cause disturbance to their current ways of doing things and they have habits luring them back to old ways of doing things. For that reason, it is very important to keep the purpose of transition in mind and have people focused on the set goals at all times. They cannot do that by simply being reminded of the purpose of change; they also need to be shown examples. Look for quick wins and use them to enforce the new ways. It is easier to move forward to bigger wins after a few smaller ones that people can use as an example of success. The beginning of a new era after a neutral phase requires consistency. To make the transition permanent, you need truthfulness, clarity, consistency and great communication. Be honest about setbacks, but at the same time keep the goal in mind and be consistent about working towards it. Make the purpose clear so that everyone involved in the transition knows why it is done.

Summary

Changes and transitions are not the same thing. Transitions are mental shifts between three different phases: old, neutral and new era. The old ways need to be removed to make way for new ones to prosper and that happens through a chaotic phase, when old dies and new is born. In an old era, the most important thing is to make the transition desirable for everyone. In a neutral phase when chaos reigns, it is good to keep focused on the goal and let the innovations flow. In the last phase of active transition management comes the new era when the old is gone and chaos starts to change into a more organised way of working. In this phase, good communication and purposeful goals are the main drivers of success.

Here are some reflective questions you can ask yourself to promote your thinking:

- What changes are happening in your organisation at the moment? Identify the different phases for them and evaluate whether there is anything that needs to be managed better.
- What transitions can you identify from in your organisation that has been successfully managed?
- What transitions have failed in your organisation? Why?
- Are goals for your transitions clear from the beginning?
- Have you made communication plans for transitions and, even more importantly, are you communicating according to them?
- How do you measure the transitions?

Write down your own thoughts here:

WEEK 50: GETTING PEOPLE TO FOLLOW YOU

The world is no longer based on a command and control style of people management, but it is based on influence and getting people to follow you voluntarily. To be able to lead people somewhere, you need to get them to follow you first. For that to happen, they need to not only listen and understand you but also to take action when needed. There are hundreds of books and techniques on how to influence people, but here we will look into powerful stories that will help you to get your point across and to get people to move in the direction you wish them to. You may think that you use strategic stories for that, but throughout history people have been inspired by paintings on cave walls, novels, movies and music that tell them something that happened to someone else and yet has relevance to their own lives. Strategies stories can help you to get your point across while having people interested in what you have to say.

However, these stories cannot simply consist of whatever comes into your mind. They need to be strategically designed to influence people in the right way. The stories need to be relevant to the topic as well as to the audience and they need to promise a better future—something they can use to see a brighter future for themselves. You want to tell them stories that move them emotionally. You need to win people's hearts. If you cannot win people's hearts, you will run into problems when obstacles and objections arise (as they always will). When crafting your stories, you need to keep in mind that it is not about you as the storyteller, but it is about the audience and what your story will move in them.

This leads to the point of the story that you will tell your audience. You need to decide what it is that you want to happen. Why should those people listening to you do something that you want them to do? Once you know the purpose of your story, you need to decide upon the positive future you want to tell them about. How will hearing this story help them to believe that taking the action will make their lives better? Then you move into the actual story, which should be told in three parts (introduction, middle and summary). Finally, after the story you will have hopefully inspired the audience enough to join you with the call for action.

Let's take an example. You are a CEO of a company who wants to change from an organisation-centric strategy to a customer-centric strategy. This will gradually cause changes to all levels of the organisation from business processes to organisational structure. Convincing the board will naturally take more than an inspiring story, but this is the first time you will be presenting this topic to them and you want them to give permission for it to proceed to the next stages. Maybe you could plan your strategic story accordingly.

The objective

Convince the management board that the customer-centric strategy is the best way for the company to succeed in the future. The desired outcome of the story is to set the company onto the path to success.

The future

Adopting a customer-centric agenda will provide the company with reduced costs, increased revenue and improved customer service. That will give the next year alone approximately 10% higher profit.

The three-part story

In the first part you could shortly present the current state of the company, which is organisation-centric and provides several hurdles for customers. The first part might also explain that the reason for this is the changed world, which has made the customers more educated and demanding. In the second part you could tell a short story about another company from the same business field that adopted customer-centric methods a few years ago and is now doing better than ever. Then in the final part you could recap the current situation of the company, how the world has changed the company, and how other companies are thriving with these new customer-centric methods.

Call for action

Once your story has (hopefully) captured the interest of the management board, you can present your proposition for moving forward, which involves asking a customer-centric consulting company to make a plan for a future roadmap and more accurate ROI calculations. Having them help your organisation will provide even more accurate estimations for the company to get the reduced costs, increased revenue and improved customer service simultaneously.

The structural layout above does not give you the exact words to say in your story. Sometimes it might be enough just to plan the overall structure, but in some cases you might want to write out the whole story and rehearse that as well as you can. When you tell stories, it is not only about the words that you say but also the body language and overall presentation skills that help you to win other people over. The greater the significance of the call for action, the more you need to practise.

Summary

Telling strategic stories is a more efficient way of getting people to follow you than showing the traditional slide presentations and fact sheets. People are intrigued by stories and they are almost always ready to hear a good story. Thus, you can use well-planned stories to make people answer your call for action. When crafting your stories, you first need to decide on the purpose of the story. Then you need to have a brighter future that is tempting to the audience. Then you should tell your story in three parts and call for action. The beauty of this approach is that it is structured and easy to use, but it is also very flexible in terms of time and needs of your audience. You can tell this kind of story in one minute or in an hour. You can craft the details and levels of facts, humour and other factors depending on who is listening.

Here are some reflective questions you can ask yourself to promote your thinking:

- Have you ever purposefully crafted the stories you tell to others?
- Do you plan for a brighter future and call for action with your stories?
- How could crafting your stories help you to get people to join the call for action easier?
- Do you know the audience you tell your stories to well enough to make it relevant?

Write down your own thoughts here:

WEEK 51: HOW TO DEAL WITH YOUR BOSS?

Employees and employers are all people. The company itself does not exist as a separate entity without people. What a company is formed of is people. I bet you have heard about those coffee table discussions where everybody rants about their bosses? Have you ever thought of how you could avoid the temptation for such a discussion? Bosses are people too you know, even though it might not always feel like that.

As long as you cannot replace your boss (with a new one or with yourself), you have to find ways to get along with him or her. You can actually improve your own job satisfaction by starting to actively manage your relationship with your boss. To start doing that, you need to first understand what kind of person your boss is. We rarely observe other people on purpose, so that is exactly what you should do. Try to understand how the boss behaves, in which situations and why. I am sure you will quickly start to find behaviour patterns that repeat themselves. Once you know that, you can start to manage it.

HR Executive Gonzague Dufour has identified seven different manager types (you might find that I use the word 'manager' here instead of 'leader' on purpose): bullies, good, kaleidoscopes, stars, scientist, navels and seventh leaders. There are other ways of understanding people types, such as the DISC profile (Dominance, Inducement, Submission and Compliance). None of these personality types are bad or good as such; they both have their places in different situations. Let's see if you can spot your boss from the list this week (the list is adapted from Dufour's book, 2011, ISBN 0071751939).

The Bully

These people are very competitive, aggressive, driven and confident. They are likely to motivate their employees with a command and conquer approach, as well as with fear and intimidation. They have no problem with questioning and ridiculing others, but they do not take criticism towards themselves lightly. So, how should you deal with such people? First, remember not to take anything they say or do personally. Try to find something positive from the situation. And if that does not help, focus solely on the professional aspects of your relationship and deal with the matters, not with emotions. Keep them informed about situations so that they get as few surprises as possible. That enables you to control the situations better because The Bully will know what is happening. Try to be as subtle as possible with these people. Behave calmly and do not get agitated. Change the ways you do this, so they cannot categorise you (to being a wimp, submissive, or such).

The Good

These managers are competent at their jobs. They believe in moderation and are patient even in stressful situations. They could be described as reasonable, efficient and stable. With the Good managers you will not get too many surprises. These people do not think outside the box or come up with wild ideas. They are easy to handle, since they avoid confrontation, but at times it might also be difficult to get them to take action. You can easily fill in the shortcomings of such managers by doing the work they ask and taking the risks they avoid. The best position for you to be with them is as their reliable sidekick they can count on. Do not play games behind their back, because they will eventually find out and remember it for a long time.

The Kaleidoscope

These managers change their personalities in a similar way that a kaleidoscope changes colours. They will behave and even talk in different ways in different situations. They are likely to treat customers, employees and other people around them in differing ways. You can expect these people to play games, manipulate and be overly self-confident. How can you handle such a person? Even though you are likely to never see the true colours of that person (since that person probably does not know it themselves), you can find out what their priorities and goals are and work towards them. You need to understand what actions you should avoid to remain in their favour. Since they often have a hidden agenda, do not focus on their words but focus on their goals. To be friends with them you should find out what kind of humour they like and indulge it.

The Star

These people love to be in the spotlight. They are dramatic and attention-seeking in one way or another. When they are not pleased with you, they will yell at you and blame you. When they are happy with you, they may present gifts and plentiful praise. It seems almost like they never run out of energy. Working with these people will mean daily highs and lows, so what you can do is to enjoy the good moments and ignore the bad ones. Since they are so high on energy, you probably cannot control them. Therefore, it is more useful to steer them in the right direction regardless of the current approach. In order to please them, you need to listen to them as they like to be in the spotlight. If you are not looking to be a star yourself, then you might fit into their team well.

The Scientist

These people like both theory and practice. They seek new information all the time and are eager to put it into practice. You will hear the latest developments from them and they are good at giving and receiving feedback. They justify their actions with knowledge, theories or systems. The downside is that they get distracted and disorganised easily. They get side-tracked and get lost there. For these reasons you can support The Scientist by giving them intellectually challenging situations. They respect reason and logic and do not appreciate sadness or anger. They will support you as long as you do not get in their way.

The Navel

The navel people are very hard to deal with, because they mainly focus on staring at their own navel. The Navels are usually very good sales people and are most successful when selling by themselves. They usually talk about matters in the first person. Navels believe in themselves so strongly that they are able to convince others to overlook their mistakes. As people, they are very action-oriented, decisive and even ruthless. They are not interested in your suggestions because they make decisions without consulting others. The bad news regarding Navels is that you cannot change their nature and you just have to deal with them. Find some way outside your working environment to vent the frustration they are causing you. To promote your career, find another boss to network with, because your advancement is not in The Navel's interest. Keep your guard up and wait for The Navel to fail and fall away.

The Seventh Leader

These are the types of managers you really want to work with. They are not promoting their own agenda, but the team's agenda. They will listen and respect you. They know that the whole is the sum of their parts. These leaders gladly receive feedback and act on it; they also give you constructive feedback. With this kind of boss, you can grow alongside them. Help to spread these good practices.

Summary

You can analyse your boss based on the Dufour's seven manager types: Bullies, Good, Kaleidoscopes, Stars, Scientist, Navels and Seventh Leaders. With Bullies, you can mention other people's strengths every now and then. With Good leaders, you can help them to take more risks: for example, by showing case examples from other companies or departments. Kaleidoscopes can easily become Seventh Leaders, so alleviate their insecurities and enforce their strengths. With Scientists, you can use other theories to open their eyes from current ones. Navels can also become Seventh Leaders, but they have the biggest change ahead of them and initiating that is not easy. Once you have gained trust from them, you can start to suggest improvements to them.

Here are some reflective questions you can ask yourself to promote your thinking:
- What kind of boss do you have?
- What kind of boss are you?
- How can you move towards becoming a Seventh leader?
- How can you become better leader?
- What kind of managers do other departments in your organisation have?

Write down your own thoughts here:

WEEK 52: HOW TO CREATE A VIRTUAL PROCESS TEAM?

Globalisation has made even locally acting companies to use resources from all over the world. For international companies, it is common practice to hold meetings and business transactions across borders and time zones. One of these contemporary phenomena is virtual process teams, in which processes are developed, analysed and executed from dispersed locations. This makes sense, since processes are the purpose for keeping those teams together. They are working together towards a common goal.

The creation of virtual process teams is useful from a profit perspective. They enable the company to reduce costs, shorten cycle times, leverage learning, and increase innovation. Virtual teams do not have to travel to the same location and if set up accordingly (for example into Europe, America, Asia and Middle East), they can work 24 hours a day. This way you do not have to pay for overtime compensation for night or holiday shifts, since you always have people available. Depending on what kind of business you are in, you can even outsource some of the time zones to subcontractors. The cycle times are shortened, since the virtual team can work on the cases all the time (when someone leaves from work, another one can continue). When people in your team work together, it enhances the exchange of learning experience and information to keep the processes flowing. That will also lead to increased innovation, since people will be figuring out how to do things in more efficient and customer-friendly ways.

In virtual process teams, sharing knowledge is very important. The use of virtual teams, provided they have the right tools supporting them, will make the most of using information. Since people are not physically located in the same place, sharing the knowledge in an effective way becomes crucial. This will also require those people to communicate with each other even more than normally, to make sure that everyone is on the same page.

Setting up virtual process teams can sometimes be hard. Some people are not used to communicating in the way that this kind of working requires. Furthermore, sometimes people fail to create personal relationships with other team members, since they might not ever meet each other face-to-face. There are some ways to alleviate this problem. You can start by creating a purpose and identity for the team. You need to be very clear about why that team exists and who they are. That will be the glue that will hold the virtual team together. This might mean that they work on certain core support processes in your company. You also need to define the milestones for the team. What exactly do they need to achieve and in what timeframe? How is this monitored and measured? Then you select the specific members for the team and each one of them needs to have a role within that team. Once the purpose, mission, goals, milestones and members of the virtual team are known, the team needs to start building the relationships. This can be done face-to-face, through conference calls and video chats. It is recommended that people talk one-to-one and also in groups. Every member should know the other members enough to communicate openly with them. Building that rapport may take some time.

Summary

Building virtual process teams may provide a company with savings. However, building those teams will take effort and time to make them work effectively. When building virtual teams, those teams need to have a clearly defined purpose, mission, goals and milestones. Even though members of the team may not ever meet each other face-to-face, it is still important to build personal relationships between the members. This may mean one-to-one and group discussions, possibly even with a facilitator.

Here are some reflective questions you can ask yourself to promote your thinking:

- Do you have functions in your organisation that could benefit from virtual teams?
- Do your customers need 24-hour access to your products or services? Would arranging virtual teams bring savings?

Write down your own thoughts here:

INDEX

ABOUT THE AUTHOR

Janne Ohtonen has over 10 years of experience in improving organisations and businesses through information technology, customer experience and process improvement projects. Janne has carried out major business development projects in the field of media, transportation, logistics, manufacturing, automotive, software development, NGOs, NPOs and management consulting. Janne has three degrees from universities, with Business Development and ICT as his major. He is currently writing a PhD thesis on Business Process Management Capabilities (BPMC). Janne also has several esteemed certifications such as The John Maxwell Team Certified Coach, Certified Process Leader, Certified Process Innovator, Certified Process Professional Master, Certified Scrum Master, Oracle Certified Enterprise Architect, and many more. Besides helping organisations to succeed through business transformation, he is also a trained business coach for leadership development. He has mentors such as the John C. Maxwell Team on his side to give him tools for top of the class leadership training. Combining leadership skills and Business Process Management tools will provide great results for any organisation looking to thrive.

This book is based on Janne Ohtonen's blogs that have been published on various prestigious blogging websites. Those articles have accumulated over 40,000 readers in under two years.

If you would like to connect with Janne Ohtonen on social media sites, you are more than welcome to do so via the following links:

LinkedIn	http://www.linkedin.com/in/janneohtonen
Facebook	http://www.facebook.com/successconsultant
Twitter	http://twitter.com/Ohtonen

Please send any feedback about this book to e-mail address: 52weeks@ohtonen.fi or send an endorsement at http://52weeks.ohtonen.fi/endorsement.html

Visit the website for this book at
http://bit.ly/52weeksbook
to get FREE infographics and videos!

TESTIMONIALS

Product Marketing and Management Professional, Managing Strategic Relationships with B2B Industry Experts/Partners

"Janne is one of the coolest but at the same time strategically inclined professionals I have worked with; he was very clear with his objectives and his requirements and this made working with him a wonderful experience. Janne also does well in assessing and sizing up those he works with and uses those assessments and conclusions for better outcomes."

Director, Lid Raisers

"I became acquainted with Janne whilst on the John Maxwell Team. I found Janne to be an innovative leader constantly looking to add value to those around him in unique ways. Janne brings refreshing ideas to coaching and I'm sure anyone looking to acquire his services will be delighted with his work. I highly recommend Janne."

Juan Rodolfo Zambrano R. Certified John Maxwell Coach, Speaker and Trainer

"Janne is a coach, speaker and trainer that has been equipped with the best material and has developed the proper skill set to work with clients one-on-one, in group settings, and through workshops and seminars to visualise, create, and execute a customised leadership strategy to best fit your needs. He has been trained by the best and I know it will show."

Senior Vice President, GLOBAL WIND LLC

"Janne is a great speaker and trainer for any organisation. He has partnered with John Maxwell who is best-known for leadership. Janne will truly be an asset to your group."

Manager, Projects, Accounts Department

"I met Janne on CPP Masters training in London. He's going to be leading CPP courses in the future and I am sure that he will be successful in that. He has carried out considerable academic research on the subject, but he remains focussed on the practical usage of Outside-In. Janne believes that Outside-In is a philosophy that is applicable internationally."

The Customer Experience Coach, Customer Experience Champion and Transformist

"I have found Janne to be enjoyable to work with, very knowledgeable and a thought leader in the areas of advanced Business Process Management (advanced BPM) and Outside-In."

Business Process Management consultant, Researcher and Team Leader

"Having worked with Janne on several projects, I have been deeply impressed by his ability to connect deeply with clients and his co-workers and his can-do positive attitude. He is also able to think in such a far-sighted manner as to separate the important from the unimportant, to effectively communicate this to all the stake-holders, and to effectively and effortlessly..."

Chief Technology Officer, Affecto Finland Oy

"Janne is a driven individual with plenty of energy and fresh new ideas. He gets things done and is excellent at finding information he needs to accomplish any task."

Account Manager, Crasman

"Janne is a skilled professional with top-quality results, a great co-worker and a friend at the same time. It's always a pleasure to work with him in the same team."

CEO/Partner, Advertising Agency Satumaa Ltd

"Janne is a true professional and a team player. He has a deep technical understanding. This is combined with open, insightful and experienced mind has always led to very fruitful results in projects."

Code Dude

"Janne is very energetic, creative, productive and a very talented person. He is highly motivated in whatever he does and gives everything his best. He brings in new ideas when needed. He has excellent analysis, design and programming skills. He also has the ability to throw doubt on bad decisions and challenge them when reasonable."

CEO, Super Analytics

"Janne is a true evangelist on his field of expertise. He is a great character and loads of fun."

Owner, doop Ltd

"Janne must be one of the most thorough people I know; he gives full attention to the task at hand and delivers very good quality work. I highly recommend Janne."

Technology Solution Professional, Microsoft

"Multi-talent developer and architect in various technologies."

Head of Capital Eastern-Central Europe, Lindorff

"We had good team spirit among us which made us efficient and created good atmosphere to our office. Janne completed every task in time and with good quality: e.g. "bug rates" were exceptionally low in every app he did. I'm happy to recommend him to join any team."

Leadership and Organisation Development Trainer, Approved supervisor and Certified Coach, Kasvupolku

"Janne can very quickly understand the clue of the problems. As a coach he works very task- and goal-oriented and in a flexible way with good listening and sharp questions. It was rewarding to work with him. I can recommend him as a Business Consult."

Legal counsel, TietoEnator Corporation

"Janne's intelligence and ability to focus is evident when being coached by him. As a co-student, one can easily notice how positive and quick in the mind Janne is. I do recommend him as a business coach."

Juan Rodolfo Zambrano R.

"This is an excellent book! Janne is a skilled consultant, speaker and coach. He has deep knowledge of improving Business Process Management (BPM) and Customer Experience Management (CEM)."

Vice President, Human Resources, Uponor Group

"I got to know Janne when we were both studying at the JTO for the certified coach training. As part of our training, Janne coached me, so I can warmly recommend him as a coach."

ADDITIONAL READING

"Outside In – The Power of Putting Customer at the Center of Your Business" by Harley manning, Amazon Publishing, 2012

"The Outside In Corporation – How to Build a Customer-centric Organization for Breakthrough Results" by Barbara E. Bund, McGraw-Hill, 2006

"Strategy from the Outside In – Profiting from Customer Value" by George S. Day, McGraw Hill, 2010

"5 Star Service – How to Deliver Exceptional Customer Service" by Michael Heppell, Pearson

"What Customers Want" by Anthony W. Ulwick, McGraw-Hill, 2005

"The DNA of Customer Experience" by Colin Shaw, Palgrave Macmillan, 2007

"What is Six Sigma Process Management? by Rowland Hayler and Michael Nichols, McGraw-Hill Companies, 2005

"Business Process Outsourcing" by Rick L. Click and Thomas N. Duening, John Wiley & Sons, Inc., 2004

"Implementing Six Sigma and Lean" by Ron Basu, Butterworth-Heineman, 2009

"What Is Lean Six Sigma?" by Bill Kastle, David Rowlands and Michael L. George, McGraw-Hill Companies, 2003

"Reawaken the Giant Within" by Anthony Robbins, Robbins Research International Inc.

"Start with Why" by Simon Sinek

"How to Win Friends and Influence People" by Dale Carnagie

AUTHOR RECOMMENDED RESOURCE: BPMLEADER.COM

BPM Leader is the largest independent community for business process management professionals worldwide. BPM Leader is the expert network and community site where you can find the latest insights, ideas and best practices on Business Process Management (BPM), Workflow Automation, Case Management (ACM), Lean Six Sigma (LSS), Change Management and related domains.

It offers a unique online platform where experts share their extensive BPM knowledge. Being a strictly independent platform, BPM Leader brings together more than 14,000 BPM professionals, bloggers, industry experts, users, vendors, consultants and analysts.

BPM Leader has awarded Janne Ohtonen a gold medal in BPM thought leadership. By September 2014 there has been over 56,000 readers for Janne Ohtonen's thought leadership on BPM Leader's website.

Visit the BPM Leader website at
http://www.bpmleader.com/author/johtonen/

AUTHOR RECOMMENDED RESOURCE: EXPOSAE.COM

Exposae believes that knowledge transfer combined with the appropriate level of consulting support is the key to producing rapid performance change plus an on-going change culture that sustains. We eat our own dog food and serve your important needs in a customer-centric way.

Our consultants and trainers are highly trained in both existing best practice approaches and the newest methods in Customer Experience Management (CEM) and advanced Business Process Management (BPM), which uncover new opportunity considerably more quickly.

We have extensive experience across a number of industries including Finance, IT, Telecoms, Education, Government, Logistics and NGOs. Our people set us apart as we provide a bespoke service in all markets and each employee is extensively trained in the Exposae BPM & CEM methodologies and tools. They are also experienced in other more traditional areas of process work including Lean Six Sigma, Enterprise Architecture and Agile methods. To complement process skills, they have advanced skills with people in addition to social and project management aspects.

Clients turn to us to help them substantially enhance their service value, increase revenues and reduce operating costs with the focus to improve the overall customer experience. We deliver superior business value by leveraging our global experts and combining our best practices, methodologies and technologies to meet their specific training and consulting needs.

Visit the Exposae website at http://exposae.com

Exposae is a brand of Magnetum Solutions Ltd.

AUTHOR RECOMMENDED RESOURCE: ADDVALUETO.ME

Have you ever participated any good business or leadership training portal? Do you think training is too expensive and takes too much time? Have you noticed that many times the training material doesn't inspire you to action? And often the methods don't bring promised value?

AddValueTo.Me is going to change all that! It has been designed to address the problems traditional online training exposes. AddValueTo.Me is a modern business and leadership portal, which has the goal of giving real value in an easy and enjoyable way. And you won't be learning alone, but joining other people who are interested about same topics and want to add value to each other!

What are the areas that you would like to develop most? Maybe you would like to be a better leader? Or to make your business more customer focused? Perhaps you want to know how to lead projects and programs more successfully?

The training programs in AddValueTo.Me are designed to give the best possible advice to your concerns. What if you had a place where you can always learn something new and ask from others how they do things successfully? And what if you had access to experienced mentors, who are eager to help you to succeed? Would that make a difference?

Why not to join for FREE and find out?

Visit the website at http://addvalueto.me

AUTHOR RECOMMENDED RESOURCE:
CAPUK.ORG

We are passionate about lifting people out of debt and poverty through our award winning debt help service and money management course, the CAP Money Course. We started in 1996 when John Kirkby gave up his successful career in consumer finance to help people out of misery and poverty associated with unmanageable debt. We have grown into a national charity with a vision to have a CAP Debt centre, opened in partnership with a local church, in every town and city across the UK.

"I am overwhelmed by what God has done. To see thousands of lives changed every year is truly wonderful. I do believe that God has given us a 21st Century answer to one of the most pressing social needs within society today. Jesus met people's needs with love, compassion and practical help. Our desire is to simply do the same and watch the miracles unfold. Please get involved in this amazing, God inspired ministry."
– John Kirkby Founder and International Director

Our services are offered totally free of charge because the people and churches who fund our work care about people in our communities who are suffering and want to help. We really do have a solution to the debt problems you are facing and it breaks our heart to know that people are going through misery when help is at hand.

Proceeds from this book are donated to CAP.

Visit the Christians Against Poverty website at https://capuk.org

AUTHOR RECOMMENDED RESOURCE:
WWW.EPMCHANNEL.COM

EPM Channel, the leading information services provider for Enterprise Performance Management, is an interactive business-to-business multi channel brand focused on the information needs of Senior Finance, FP&A, Strategy, Decision Support, BI, and Compensation executives, with an emphasis on gaining widespread EPM adoption and engagement throughout the organization.

We understand the real-world challenges confronting organizations and provide the intelligence needed to stay current and to compete effectively. In addition to providing on-demand thought leadership and core strategies for improving enterprise performance management, we also offer benchmark data, analytic tools, and peer-to-peer networks to deliver unparalleled, actionable insights.

Specialties:

Performance Management, FP&A, Forecasting, Operational Planning, Strategy Development & Execution, Business Forecasting, Pay for Performance, Business Analytics, Business Intelligence, Integrated Business Planning and Social Media Analytics.

Visit the EPM Channel website at www.EPMChannel.com

AUTHOR RECOMMENDED RESOURCE:
WWW.EBCG.COM

B2B is history! We create a fresh H2H - Human 2 Human event experience for you! Our Vision is to create opportunities where world-changing ideas are inspired.

Our Mission is to become the preferred partner for boosting business potential via innovative conferences and trainings created with passion. Most of all, we want you to love working with EBCG and to enjoy the entire experience. Our focus is for that passion to be reflected in your real results.

If you are looking for an interactive course which would enhance desired business skills or provide you with a practical roadmap to solve a concrete issue, then our in-depth trainings and workshops are the perfect solution for you.

In cooperation with top trainers and influencers, we can provide you with advanced training solutions in the areas like negotiation, public speaking, charisma, communication or leadership and a number of workshops focused on trending industry topics.

Nothing beats the experience of meeting people face-to-face to gain inspiration, to learn, and to do business. You can expect to come away from an EBCG event with (at the very least) a couple of big ideas, several new key contacts, and more than a few high quality business leads.

That's how we contribute to the business communities we serve, and how you gain a serious competitive advantage.

Visit the EBCG website at www.ebcg.com

FREE VIDEOS AND INFOGRAPHICS

GET FREE VIDEOS AND INFOGRAPHICS AT

http://bit.ly/52weeksbook

GIVE ENDORSEMENTS FOR THIS BOOK AT

http://52weeks.ohtonen.fi/ endorsement.html